THE *Badass* WITHIN

STORIES OF STRENGTH, HOPE AND COURAGE

Liz Benecke-Wipfli, Sarah Cozzini, Emily Mckissick Diaz, Sydney Jackson-Clockston, Janet Langmeier, Coral Laski, Caroline Lemieux, Erica B. Lopez, Melissa Mae, Nicole J. Nohl, Susan Paxson, Marie-anne Rouse, Karen Siliven-Monnier, Kim Bark White

FOREWORD BY DR. SHELLIE HIPSKY

Copyright © 2022 by Erin Baer.

All rights reserved. No part of this publication may be reproduced, distributed, or transmitted in any form or by any means, including photocopying, recording, or other electronic or mechanical methods, without the prior written permission of the publisher, except in the case of brief quotations embodied in critical reviews and certain other noncommercial uses permitted by copyright law. For permission requests, contact the publisher at the website address below.

Author: Erin Baer.

Website: https://beatentobadass.com/

Publisher: Beaten To Badass

The Badass Within / Erin Baer. First edition.

The information contained in this book is for general information and entertainment purposes only. The recommendations, opinions, experiences, observations, or other information contained herein is provided "as is" and neither the author nor publisher make any representations or warranties of any kind, express or implied, about the accuracy, suitability, reliability, or completeness of this book's content. Any reliance a reader places on such information is therefore strictly at their own risk. All recommendations are made without guarantee on the part of the author and publisher. To the maximum extent permitted by law, the author and publisher disclaim all liability from this publication's use. In no event will either author or publisher be liable to any reader for any loss or damage whatsoever arising from the use of the information contained in this book. This book is not a substitute for professional services, and readers are advised to seek professional aid in the event of an emergency.

ISBN: 979-8-218-06440-2

PRAISE

The amazing author of *From Beaten To Badass* has done it again! Erin Bear brings us *The Badass Within*. The amazing women in this book share stories that are tough, hopeful and relatable. Every person who is struggling to find their badass within needs this book.

This is a book that I will keep on the shelf for the times when I need to gather courage and strength. Get ready to be inspired …

— Colette Smith

The challenging, devastating, yet courageous true life stories of 15 women is inspiring! Their stories keep you in suspense and give you a first-hand look at how they fought their fight to overcome and survive. Can't say enough about the raw emotion that I felt reading each story.

— Billiejo Hyer

Heart breaking to heart warming. Struggling to strength. Raw and restrained to resilient. Suffering to survivor.

Beautifully written and eloquently articulated stories that struck chords within my soul. These women's stories ignited my inner fire of badassery. For so long, I have felt so alone in my own journey. I used to hear other women's stories and feel that my own story wasn't "as bad" as others. While I am proud of the mountains I have climbed over, I never felt as worthy of the same praise as others. Until this book. About halfway through, the proverbial lightbulb flickered on. It doesn't matter the experiences we have been through. Iit matters what we do with it, how we handle it, how we grow, how we embrace our inner badass. And how we hold our heads high and walk into the storm with fire in our eyes and scream, "I am worthy! Watch me be the Badass I am."

—Danielle Danforth

These are some brave individuals that have bared their struggles, pain and sorrow. They have found ways to work through that and have become better people. You are not alone! Find YOUR badass within!

— Kim S.

What an amazing way to inspire others to never stop believing in themselves, to always keep going, and never ever feel like they're alone. Every story sheds light on the fact that each day is a new day, and to never ever take it for granted.

— Missy Cornwell-Nichols

The *Badass Within* is a beautiful collaboration among women who are courageous enough to be vulnerable and open with their audience, with a united goal of helping others. While each of their stories is unique, the common theme of strength, perseverance, and never giving up is present throughout and everyone can find a story to relate to.

— Vanessa Rush, Ph.D.

From the first story to the last story, The Badass Within is a powerful read. I was crying, shouting, praying and cheering these ladies on as I was drawn into their amazing, powerful and challenging lives. They all have faced adversities that would have crippled most people but they dug deep within themselves and moved forward. From addiction, mental, physical abuse and illness, unhealthy marriages and even death, they knew they had something in them that said "Don't Give Up" and they didn't, even when others tried to hold them back. I pray I don't have to face any situation remotely similar but if I do, I will turn to them for their message of hope.

—Beth Bilton

DEDICATION

To all those who have found themselves in the storms of life, looking for the light to find they are not alone. May the stories within this book give you hope, strength, and courage to become your own hero as you find the *badass* within.

CONTENTS

Foreword xi

Why the Elephant? xiii

What Is a Badass? xv

Introduction 1

Erin Baer
I Am My Body's Keeper 5

Liz Benecke-Wipfli
Forget Normal 15

Sarah Cozzini
Divorcing Alcohol 25

Emily Mckissick Diaz
Bloody, But Unbowed 31

Sydney Jackson-Clockston
Uprooting Negative Self-Talk 41

Janet Langmeier
You Complete Me 51

Coral Laski
Getting Out Of My Own Way 59

Caroline Lemieux
UNFUCKWITHABLE 69

Erica B. Lopez
Surviving my Mother's Death 81

Melissa Mae
Sucker Punched 93

Nicole Nohl
Embrace The Barefoot Moments.......................................103

Susan Paxson
Lizard Brain and Wizard Brain..111

Marie-anne Rouse
Nobody Knew 121

Karen Siliven-Monnier
One Step At A Time..129

Kim Bark White
Roller Coaster Ride of Grief 139

In Gratitude...149

About the Author..153

Connect with Erin 155

FOREWORD

The *Merriam-Webster Dictionary* defines the word "badass" in two ways…

badass
adjective bad·ass \-ˌas\

Definition of *BADASS*
1. *often vulgar:* ready to cause or get into trouble
2. *often vulgar:* of formidable strength or skill

WHILE READING THIS IMPACTFUL BOOK compendium spearheaded by Erin Baer, *The Badass Within*, I originally thought the title was referring to the second definition. After all, the authors shine with their skill in writing their powerful stories and they demonstrate time and time again their strength of heart and mind, and at times their physical conquering of that which was ailing them.

However, after finishing the book, I clearly see the first definition shining through. Rep. John Lewis, who devoted his life to equality and justice for all, stated, "Good trouble, necessary trouble—it's not only OK, but necessary to enact and inspire meaningful change." The stories in this book often describe getting into good trouble in a badass way to change the trajectory of the authors' lives, thereby giving hope to readers for their own lives.

Erin Baer is a true badass, making a profound difference in the world by telling her truth and shining a spotlight on others who are badass as well. We must all speak our truth to help others who are in darkness.

Over a dozen empowered women in this book pour into their readers with hope and emotion. I encourage you to read their stories and tell your own badass stories as well. Because as I always say, "Inspiration is just a story away!"

—Dr. Shellie Hipsky, The Global Empowerment Coach, CEO of Inspiring Lives International, and Executive Director of The Global Sisterhood

WHY THE ELEPHANT?

ELEPHANTS HAVE ALWAYS BEEN my favorite animal. The majestic yet giant creature shows such strength and power in all of its wonder. Yet, with their size they are still sensitive, wise, stable, intelligent, loyal, peaceful, reliable, and determined in all that they do. I feel a connection to the qualities that the elephant has and only hope to be as majestic while living a life of integrity and confronting the "elephants in the room."

Elephants also never forget, in the same way I have never forgotten. I continue to move forward, learning from my past, embracing my present, and looking toward my future with the patience that these gentle giants possess.

Erin Baer

WHAT IS A BADASS?

LIFE WAS NEVER PROMISED to be easy. Honestly, if it were, it would be boring. However, we never know what this life of ours is going to throw at us, we just know it's the journey that teaches us who we are, who we have been, and who we want to be. There are many peaks and valleys along the way and sometimes everything seems to be smooth and easygoing. Other times, we take shortcuts and detours, and we feel as if we go one step forward and two steps back. Those circumstances that knock us down will either keep us down or allow us to find the strength to rise. It's in all those moments we either let the hard times define us when we are bruised, broken, and feeling defeated, or we choose to get back up.

Some of those moments make us feel like life has beaten us down, whether it was in school, at work, or abuse by parents, by bullies, or by beating ourselves up. Some of those moments are traumas we have survived, such as illness, grief, or health issues that knock us down; anything that's beaten us down in life.

But we can still get up. Circumstances don't have to define us. We can make the choice to live the life that we want to live regardless of what's happened in the past. That's a decision we have to make. I want you to know that you are not the only one who has been through it, regardless of what has happened. If you're like me, you started believing you weren't good enough or what you did didn't seem good enough. No matter how hard you've been beaten down, you can still be a *badass* because it's already in you. You just have to make the choice to be that *badass* yourself. Your scars are beautiful, they don't define you—they are lines on the roadmap to your true passion. What God intended you to do. You have a *badass within*. It's time to unleash her and share her with the world.

INTRODUCTION

WHEN I WROTE MY FIRST BOOK, *From Beaten to Badass,* I had no idea the impact that my story about surviving domestic abuse and other challenges would make around the world. I just knew that my story needed to be shared and my hope was if it could help just one person it was all worth it.

Within the first year, I quickly realized that my book could help so many more that have experienced similar challenges. I soon set out on a mission to get copies of my book into shelters across the US. This became known as the ***Make an Impact Mission****.* I began sharing my story and mission on social media, podcasts, and magazine articles hoping others could see how they too could make a difference in the lives of others by sponsoring a book and being the light in the darkness for survivors. Then COVID-19 hit in 2020, and I was more determined to shine a light on the darkness of abuse, to get more books into shelters, and be the hope that so many needed.

During 2020, over 500 shelters were sponsored, and survivors of all walks of life were receiving strength, hope, and courage when they needed it most, in those dark moments of isolation when all they could do was survive.

I started receiving letters and messages about how important it was that I was sharing my story. It gave others courage to stand up for themselves and begin sharing their stories. My story helped them realize they too were *badasses*. The **Make an Impact Mission** is still going strong today.

From there, I wanted to do more and was soon invited to be part of several book collaborations where I could share other personal stories.

I then thought to myself, "Maybe I could create a book collaboration of authors and invite them to share their stories of how they overcame, persevered and became the *badasses* they were always meant to be." As with anything new that pushes you out of your comfort zone, the doubt and fear set in.

I began telling myself things that were in fact just not true.

It's not the right time. You're not worthy. No one will believe you. The work you want to do is too hard, you'll never succeed. You won't make the impact you are hoping for. You'll be forgotten.

Then I realized I had to reframe my self-doubt and realize that not only can I do it, but I also *need* to do it. I changed the script and decided to take action and create a space where women can share their stories and empower others.

I began telling myself, "The timing couldn't be any better. I am more than worthy because I determine my worth. People will believe me because I am honest. I don't care how hard the work is going to be, I will be successful. I will make an impact because I already have. I am unforgettable because I have already put my mark on this world and it's time to help others do the same."

I knew there were women out there that were inspired to share their stories and have their voices be heard. They just needed the space, and so I spearheaded that project. I put a post on Facebook and asked for those who wanted to share their story in written form. As soon as I hit enter, I had several women raise their virtual hand and say "Me!"

INTRODUCTION

The Badass Within book project was born. Fifteen women including myself share parts of our lives with the world for the first time as we tear down our walls and become vulnerable through our words.

Everyone has an "elephant in the room" and we tend to turn our backs to it rather than turning around, confronting the elephant and helping it out the door. However, as we decide to turn and look at the elephant, we realize it is not the elephant that is the problem, it is what the elephant represents, what it reflects, and what it is chained to. As humans, it is impossible to go through this life without getting beat up, going through a life-changing event, and being changed because of it. Yet, we don't seem to want to talk about it and instead we let the elephant stay in the room, ignored.

My purpose in life is to not only confront the elephants in the room, but to love the elephant, to realize it is there in the room waiting to be freed.

The stories in this book are personal, real, and courageous. The women have shared something they never thought they could. Yet they chose to share their stories with the world so they too can free their elephants.

I invite you to go on this journey, read the stories of these *badass* women, and be inspired about how courageously and vulnerably they live. Through their stories you will witness sadness, joy, and strength. My hope is that you also reflect on your life and the experiences you have gone through, and realize you too have a *badass within*.

Erin Baer

I AM MY BODY'S KEEPER

"When it comes to your health, the biggest advocate for your own treatment and care should be you."
—Sara Gottfried MD, Author of the *Hormone Cure*

How could you do this? I don't get it, haven't I treated you well, and haven't I always looked out for you and me? After all, we are supposed to be a team! My own body, how dare you betray me!

HERE I AM, THIRTY-NINE YEARS OLD, and I feel like a stranger in my own body. *How did I get here?* As I replay the last six years over and over in my brain, "I feel betrayed by my own body as it wreaked havoc on itself. I feel even more betrayed by the healthcare system. I feel as though I am watching from the sidelines as the devastation occurs within my body."

Thirty pounds overweight! How did this happen? I have always been healthy, and I take pride in what I feed my body and my mind: exercising, eating well, and if I didn't feel right, I went to the doctor. That all made sense and seemed to be working… and then I wanted a baby.

I thought it would be easy. I thought I would get pregnant, and all would be okay. In 2016, I retired from competitive bodybuilding and hung up the sparkly, five-inch heels, thinking I was trading them in for ten little toes, ten little fingers, and a cute button nose. But after eighteen months of trying, the trade wasn't coming through. Then questions flooded my mind. *What was wrong with me? What was wrong with my husband?* We met with a fertility specialist, thinking that the doctor could fix it all. Little did I know, it was the beginning of a journey I wasn't prepared for. A journey of doors opening, only for them to be slammed shut, only to realize that there was nothing on the other side, and looking for another door once again. I have been through so many doors that led to rooms I wish I had never been in. Rooms that led to loss, heartbreak, and surgeries.

To give you some insight to our plight, I have endured two ectopic pregnancies,[1] one in 2018 and the second in 2019, which resulted in the loss of two of my angel babies.

The second pregnancy loss hit me even harder than the first one for a couple of reasons. One, I had not realized I was pregnant. Two, suffering acute pain, I thought I was experiencing a ruptured ovarian cyst.

I was taken to the emergency room where I learned I was pregnant. And the pregnancy was ectopic, which meant I would lose the baby. I was reeling from this news when the doctors gave me two choices to save my life: be injected with methotrexate as a means of resolving "the issue" or have surgery.

This emergency department was not equipped to perform surgery, so I was discharged and sent to another hospital. Now, in a second emergency room, I

---

1   An ectopic pregnancy is when gestation occurs elsewhere than in the uterus (as in a fallopian tube or in the peritoneal cavity). *Merriam-Webster's Unabridged Dictionary*, Merriam-Webster, accessed May 31, 2022, https://unabridged.merriam-webster.com/unabridged/ectopic%20pregnancy.

received the same choices. However, this emergency room physician was very insistent that methotrexate injection was the simpler and quicker solution.

Here is where my intuition spoke to me, and I insisted that my fertility doctor be contacted before a decision on treatment moved forward.

The emergency room physician and I were not seeing eye to eye on the surgery option, but he did admit that the female reproductive system was out of his realm of specialization. Although he continued to insist that the methotrexate would be sufficient, I solidly refused. I knew I had felt an explosion inside of me and I gave him the rundown about my loss from the 2018 ectopic pregnancy that resulted in two doses of methotrexate and surgery—neither treatment on its own resolved the issue. Finally, he hesitantly listened to me and called my fertility clinic. My fertility doctor, having intimate knowledge of my previous pregnancy and medical history, advised me to undergo the emergency surgery.

After that, the emergency room doctor decided to get the ob–gyn doctor who was upstairs delivering a baby to come down as soon as she finished to assess me. She came in, evaluated me, and looked at the notes in my chart. However, not all the notes were uploaded yet from the first hospital, and I insisted that she too call my fertility specialist. She did. The next thing I knew, she was in my room and telling me she had one job, *to save my life*. My life was saved, but I lost my baby, my fallopian tube, and I lost so much more.

The wonderful doctor who saved my life in December 2019 is now my ob–gyn. She told me after the surgery that it was too risky and dangerous for me to try to conceive naturally or through IUI (intrauterine insemination). She told me right before I went back for surgery that my only option to conceive would be in vitro fertilization (IVF). That news was a terrible blow.

As I healed from the surgery, my heart kept breaking. I would randomly cry for no reason, I felt down, and I had more questions than answers about why all this was happening. Not to mention, I now had two angel babies that I never got to meet. Not yet anyway.

During my post-op appointment in January 2020, my doctor had a heart-to-heart conversation that opened my eyes to why I felt so hopeless. She told me I was struggling with postpartum depression (PPD). I was confused. I thought you had to have a baby to suffer from PPD. I was wrong. Not only did I just lose a baby, but I had also lost one a year prior and never grieved that loss. I now was grieving the loss of both babies, my tube, and the ways I could never conceive. After all, I only had one option left: IVF.

I didn't know what to do or how to move forward. My doctor suggested therapy to help me navigate my postpartum depression and talk through all the things when it came to my personal journey of infertility. I honestly just wanted it to all go away and wake up in hopes it was just a dreadful nightmare. Yet I was in the middle of it all, as I felt it deep in my soul. I was more lost than ever, and I needed help. I needed someone to be on my side, to listen to me, support me, and help me become my body's keeper. Therapy made the most sense amid the chaos of all the loss I was experiencing. I didn't know how to grieve. I had never experienced such a loss before, and this loss knocked the breath right out of me. I felt hopeless, helpless, and frozen. So, I took a step into the unknown world of postpartum depression and allowed my therapist to lead the way.

When the COVID-19 pandemic hit us, the world was in a frenzy. However, for me, the pandemic was a blessing in disguise. It helped me focus on my therapy and health, and to understand the inner workings of my mind, soul, and heart. Though therapy moved from in-person to online, it was much needed. I wasn't about to abandon myself.

My husband and I decided with our most recent loss, I needed to heal, focus on me, and stay well with the pandemic in full swing. It made it easy to choose me and to put the idea of having a family on hold, at least for now.

I worked hard in therapy. I cried, I laughed, I hoped, I cried some more. My therapist helped me realize I was to be in charge, not the doctors. I needed to be leading my health, and make the decisions that are best for me, not the other way around. As I grieved my two losses, I found a little bit of hope and began to open my heart up to the possibility of pursuing IVF.

As 2020 came to a close, my husband and I discovered that a New York fertility clinic we were considering traveling to was opening an office in Colorado. Instead of jetting off to New York, I just had to make a trip two hours each way. We were so excited, because that meant we could pursue IVF close to home. To make things even better, this clinic offered it at a third of the cost of other places, so it was affordable. My hope grew a little more. I set up a video consultation, and on that call, learned I was a perfect candidate for IVF. I was overjoyed.

The next step was to wait for my menstrual cycle to start, to call the clinic, and go in for my ultrasound and blood work. *Woohoo! It is all really happening!* My period showed up, I called, and I went to my first appointment. I was excited, nervous, and every other emotion came flooding through. I was given the green light, it was time! The first step to IVF is growing those eggs.

I made my payment and ordered all my medications. The box arrived. Talk about overwhelming! But to me it was like Christmas. After all, I was hopeful that I would be counting ten little toes and ten little fingers by the end of 2021.

For the next thirteen days, I took medications, suppositories, and shots, all in hopes of retrieving a good number of high-quality eggs.

January 8, 2021 was egg retrieval time. The doctor put me under anesthesia and retrieved the eggs. When I woke up, they informed me there were fourteen eggs in my basket, waiting to be fertilized. We ended up with six fertilized eggs, which we opted to get tested to make sure that we gave ourselves and our embryos the best shot of having a healthy baby. The egg retrieval was hard on me and my body. Something wasn't right, and I was in excruciating pain. On January 9, 2021, I called the doctor and was advised to go to the emergency room.

I explained my pain to the ER doctor, and he did nothing. This was the same doctor who almost let me die two years prior. I was looking at this doctor, who thinks he knows more than the patient in front of him because of the letters that follow his name, and I demanded he call that fertility clinic that just performed the egg retrieval, and he did. However, he didn't do as they said. Instead of giving me the four medications my fertility specialist advised him to give me, he prescribed me medication for anxiety. *After all, I am a female so I must be exaggerating.* I went home in hopes my pain would subside and eventually go away. It didn't.

The pain was so bad that thirty-six hours later—I was back in the same emergency room. This time, the nurse who had helped me the day before told the doctor on duty that evening that I was truly in immense pain and that they needed to get it under control. They ran a bunch of tests, got my pain under control, and sent me home.

As I was healing, I was on bedrest and four weeks flew by. Finally, the embryo test results came back, and I was hopeful. The hope didn't last long as I received another blow and was devastated to learn that only two embryos were viable. I had more grieving to do. Little did I know, my journey was about to get even harder.

Forget about all the drugs, injections, and IVF appointments. Listening to my body and advocating for my health was the hardest part. I took most of 2021 off of work and allowed my body, mind, and heart to heal once more. Throughout the summer I regained my health, lost some weight, and I felt unstoppable. So I knew it was time to do our first IVF transfer. It was scheduled and took place the day after Thanksgiving. I had so much hope. The transfer went smoothly, and the waiting began. After one week, I had an appointment to check my numbers. My blood work showed a drop, and I just knew the transfer didn't work. It was confirmed a week later. Three losses. Three angel babies. And more grieving.

I had a medical consultation and found myself once more needing to advocate for my health before moving forward. I opted to have a diagnostic surgery on December 21, 2021. The results all came back normal, except two crucial tests. The first test was for the BCL6 protein, which if abnormally high, makes IVF transfer success highly unlikely. Even if it does work at first, it usually fails, eventually resulting in miscarriage. This was the case for me. The second test was the Receptiva®, a test to show the exact window of implantation for IVF. So again, I advocated for my health. As I spoke to the doctor about these results, I asked what I could do. Another surgery was suggested. I said *yes*!

I had surgery on February 25, 2022, to diagnose and treat endometriosis, while also removing the remaining fallopian tube to prevent any future complications. Following my surgery, I was put into medical menopause. This meant four different medications and no period. *Woohoo! What could go wrong?* Everything.

The first few weeks were smooth. I was healing from surgery and taking it easy. Then, bam! It all hit me like a brick wall. Chronic pain, difficulty walking or sitting, difficulty doing most things. *Make it stop, just make it all stop. I can't take it anymore and I refuse to go on like this. This is not living, this is not me, this is not my body*. I started crying out for help. After all, I am my body's keeper.

I was on four different medications, and they were destroying my body. I was on human growth hormone (HGH) injections, supplements to enhance natural production of HGH, and two other medications to stop menstruation, which put me into medical menopause. After three weeks of these medications, my body began adding more weight, retaining fluid, and hurting in every joint. My hands and fingers would go numb, my feet wouldn't support my weight, and every step I took felt like I was walking on lava rocks. After a month of chronic pain, I called my doctor and demanded answers (nicely, of course).

This is when I began to advocate assertively for my health and demand answers until I got them.

I begged for them to change the medication doses, and they agreed. First, the nurse told me I shouldn't be in this much pain, so she reduced the HGH medications and told me to give it time and look for improvements. I had a little relief, but then my knee began to hurt more, and the fluid wasn't going away. I called my doctor's office again, and they decided to reduce my other two medications.

I was starting to feel empowered. *Finally, just maybe, I will start feeling better.* The swelling was going down slightly, but I was still in extreme pain, and I could barely walk. This was making life miserable. I called my doctor again and explained my symptoms. Finally, they decided I needed to stop the HGH medications. I felt like I had finally been heard and was hopeful the pain would disappear. I was wrong.

My hip began to hurt and made it impossible to walk, my feet hurt, I still had swelling all over, and the weight wasn't budging. I was exhausted from it all. I felt like my body had completely betrayed me again. *Or was it me betraying my body?* I just wanted it all to stop. I prayed they would let me stop the rest of my meds.

Once again, I called the fertility clinic and went through all my symptoms. As the nurse spoke, I wasn't sure if I heard her right. She told me I shouldn't be in this much pain, and the best thing to do was to stop all the medications. I asked, "Did you say that I could stop all meds?" She gave me a resounding yes! Finally, advocating for my health and my body paid off.

I am still recovering from the chronic pain that two months of these medications caused. It's not all gone. However, I feel hopeful because now I can truly begin my recovery after everything my body has been through. From the losses, the surgeries, the medications, the weight gain, and everything in between, I can now close the door of infertility and open a new door to whatever the future holds. By the time you read this I will have gone through one more surgery in July 2022, a hysterectomy. I can't tell you how I feel about it, because at the time of writing of this it hasn't happened yet. What

I can tell you is that it's not a surgery I want, but it is a surgery I need for my overall health and quality of life. If I have learned anything on this journey, it is that I am to advocate for my health first because I am my body's keeper.

Being an advocate for one's own health is empowering; however it doesn't make decision-making easier. If anything, I think it makes it more difficult. For example, having to make the most difficult decision to have a hysterectomy for my overall health was painful. It was one decision I didn't want to have to make, but also one I needed to make so I could finally resolve a lot of my health issues. When it comes to your health, you must be your own advocate. You must do what's right for you, not what anyone else is telling you whether it's family, friends, and health professionals. Doing your research, asking questions, and sitting with the information helps, but ultimately you need to do what's right for you. I encourage you to listen to your body, advocate for you and your body, and remember you are your body's keeper and that is *badass*!

About Erin

ERIN BAER, founder of Beaten to Badass, is herself a survivor of domestic violence and sexual assault. Her organization, Beaten to Badass, is dedicated to empowering women to become their own heroes.

Erin began telling others her story of grace and grit on her road to recovery. This sharing of her personal story became the basis for her first book, *From Beaten to Badass*. This powerfully worded personal memoir gives readers the strength, hope, and courage to keep going and become the *badass* they were always meant to be.

Seeing women being silenced for wanting to be strong, courageous, and proud of who they are while moving on from feeling beaten down by life, Erin decided to be a positive voice providing an example that circumstances do not define us and that we too can be our own heroes. Through her writing, coaching, and speaking, Erin encourages women to look within where they will find their power to unleash the *badass within*.

If you are feeling defeated, or feel life is unfair by the cards you were dealt, the only way you lose is if you don't learn and you don't get back up. **You are a badass!**

Erin is now a thriving entrepreneurial badass who lives her passions as a best-selling Author, Speaker, and Coach. She has contributed to many book collaborations, including *Hold My Crown, Overcoming Heart Blocks,* and *Healing and Growth* (releasing in December 2022). As with all of Erin's projects, a portion of the proceeds go to empowering women's charities.

CONNECT WITH ERIN

- ErinBaer.com and BeatentoBadass.com
- Facebook: erinbaerbadass and beatentobadass
- Instagram: coach_erinbaer and beatentobadass
- LinkedIn: erinbaerbadass
- Linktr.ee/erinbaer

Liz Benecke-Wipfli

FORGET NORMAL

I JUST WANTED TO BE "normal." Don't we all? Well, I'm here to tell you there is no such thing as normal. Stop trying to find it! Chasing normal destroyed my life, and I didn't even realize it. Not to mention I have no idea whose definition of normal I was even chasing.

My birth mother was very ill when I was young. My sister and I were placed into a foster family states away in Wisconsin. After my mother passed, we were adopted. Our new adopted family sent my sister back to south Florida where she was raised by our Granny. That began my journey being raised as an only child.

I heard a million people with siblings tell me how lucky I was to be an only child. They had no idea how badly I longed for a sibling to combat the loneliness I felt every single day growing up. That's when the anxiety, depression, and acting out started. I was flat-out a jerk! I desperately needed some professional help, but my parents took matters into their own hands. While I think that my adopted parents loved me in their own weird way, their choices haunted me into adulthood.

In many ways, I was completely out of control and threw some pretty incredible tantrums. No one ever asked me what was wrong. No one ever taught me how to communicate appropriately. No one taught me appropriate ways to get out the excessive energy of ADHD, combined with singleton boredom. No one taught me boundaries.

I was constantly compared to a "well-behaved" cousin. But I was mostly subjected to confinement and submission. I was literally pinned in place whenever they didn't like something I did, sat on so I couldn't move. Dumping water on my face was another routine punishment. Sometimes I had to eat soap or hot sauce or got dragged down the hall by my limbs. Being confined and sat on was nearly a daily occurrence. I begged to be let go. The more I begged, the longer they'd sit on me. The longer I was confined, the more my behavior escalated. This vicious cycle continued into my teens.

I only had friends over to our house two times. My parents knew I was so lonely, but if I had gotten on medication or had seen a counselor, they'd have to admit that I was not perfect. My mother's favorite show was *Keeping Up Appearances* on BBC. You better believe my parents tried their best to hide my issues, and to get me to conform to the "normal" behavior that they expected of me.

My teen years began, and I went to every camp, sport, and activity that I possibly could just to stay away from the house. Frequently, I surfed my friends' couches. And still an epic failure in my parents' eyes because the majority of my friends were guys. I had zero desire to learn about makeup when I could ride ATVs and play in the mud. But the accusations about my involvement with them began to fly; I should have girlfriends to hang out with. I wasn't actually doing anything sexual. But as it continued, I, in all my teenage brilliance, decided to defy them in protest. I had no sense of love and belonging. So I thought sex might be good. Then I was pregnant at fifteen. Two months after my sixteenth birthday, I had my first son.

Motherhood. Oh my. *How can this girl who literally doesn't know how to boil water keep a tiny human alive?* Since I had such a stellar personality and no idea how to maintain a friendship, much less a long-term relationship, my son's dad and I had split prior to his birth. I was alone. I hated being alone. So I found an older guy, and that relationship was not good. I was alone again. *Now what do I do?* Working for minimum wage at a grocery store wasn't going to pay the bills. After a failed attempt in the military because of my body not being able to withstand the onslaught and it fell apart, I enrolled in nursing school and worked as a server at a few of the local establishments. I struggled.

I wanted to be in school, but I just couldn't focus. At eighteen, my ADHD was finally addressed. Then school was amazing! I enjoyed all of the people that I worked with and got my first apartment. I was doing it! Except that childcare was so expensive. My mom didn't work but was a preschool teacher for twenty years previously. She offered to help. Then the rules for my son started.

They said I either did it their way or I wouldn't get help. I was more than willing to be reasonable but there were absolutely no boundaries with them, and they didn't respect the things I wanted for my child. Still a girl with few skills, what was I supposed to do? Even though I moved into my own home, I began having the feelings of worthlessness again.

Feeling like I was missing out on life, I went to a friend's college graduation party and tried to play catch up. I caught up all right. I couldn't drive so I asked my friend if I could stay at his house. He obliged, and another one of his friends stayed as well. These were guys I knew and should have been safe with. Little did I know, I was as far from safe with these guys. I really liked one guy and had a little make-out session with him. It was wonderful. Then our other friend got out of the shower. That's when they told me that since that night I walked into a bar wearing a cute shirt and my khaki capris, they had decided they wanted to share me. I was not into that in the slightest. I attempted to get up and leave. That's when they raped me. I was already in a constant downward spiral with my not-so-fantastic choices. Now I was a complete train wreck.

I had this complete derailment of my life, and I told no one. I didn't feel I had anyone in my life that I could confide in. So I buried it as deep down as I could. Consequential mistake. I spent the next ten plus years of my life trying to gain back control.

I had my second son at nineteen and my third son at twenty-one. I got married, graduated nursing school, and began my graduate bridge program for my master's degree in nursing. Life was good. Not really. But I did an outstanding job of continuing to hide my pain from the general population. I was still experiencing severe anxiety, depression, and occasional sudden outbursts when I couldn't get my anxiety under wraps. I did go on a mild antidepressant, but I didn't know exactly what I was feeling, so I failed to let my doctor know how debilitating life could be for me at times. I certainly didn't share my "dirty secret" with him.

I had a great job as a nurse manager. My family was starting to get financially balanced, which included allowing us to enjoy more things. I was starting to feel better. My anxiety seemed to be decreasing substantially. I gave horse riding lessons to folks with disabilities, and I was loving being a hockey mom. My cup was looking pretty full. Hallelujah! But it didn't last long.

My husband and I got divorced. It was anything but pretty. There was so much hurt; no more love and belonging. I allowed the negative cycles to begin yet again. I went through cops, EMTs, firefighters, farriers, engineers, military personnel, you name it. If a man showed me an ounce of interest, I was convinced I was going to marry them so everything could be okay again. I had my baby girl during this cycle and then found a guy, moved out of state, and thought everything was awesome. I didn't recognize the postpartum depression that I was displaying, I just knew that something wasn't right. When I discussed it with my doctor, I was definitely more honest than before, and started to take medication that addressed both depression and anxiety. At the same time, I injured my back and started on prednisone to decrease the swelling.

Unloading hay for my horses, I suddenly went from fine to psychotic. I jumped on an ATV and drove like a crazy person (I was a crazy person at that point). Paranoid, I thought my son was trying to murder me. I was screaming, not recognizing people, and being completely unreasonable. (I was told all this, as I don't remember much of the event myself.) The cops came, took me to the emergency room, and I agreed to go for further treatment at an inpatient mental health hospital. I didn't understand what was going on with my body. At the mental hospital, I colored a lot, participated in group therapy at a mediocre level at best, met a new guy, and then left after realizing that what caused my problems was a reaction to the prednisone.

When I got home, all of my stuff was packed into garbage bags, my animals were surrendered to the humane society, and my children had been taken back to Wisconsin in the few days that I was in the hospital. I got ahold of everyone and made plans to get everything sorted out. My kids were with friends who had offered to help. I hadn't ever been a person to show much weakness, so I was accepting help from others for the first time.

I needed to get all of our belongings back to Wisconsin to find a new job and a new place for us to live. I didn't want to have to drag my kids through all of these tedious processes. My friends called me a week later, and they met me at the park with my kiddos. That's when they presented me with temporary custody paperwork. I declined. These were my kids. I had asked for some help. I didn't want to get rid of my children. They were my babies. "They're not going anywhere."

That's when the true definition of train wreck began.

I went to pick my son up at school and he wasn't there. The school stated that my friend had picked him up an hour before. Then they told me that the kids were at the police department. I called an attorney who told me to go get my kids, that they couldn't hold them like that. But it was too late. They were in protective custody. The only thing I was told was a court date.

I was always a hot mess, but this was a level of anxiety I had never experienced. *Don't mess with my kids!* I went to the crisis center because I didn't know what else to do. I was homeless at this point, I had seventeen legal documents of allegations against me, and I could do nothing other than pray. The people that I did have a sense of love and belonging with were the ones who said terrible things about me; some were true, but some were so far from the truth I couldn't even believe it was said.

During the ten months that my children were away, I not only fought to get them back, but I also fought for myself. It was time to get control of the mess I called my life. The single hardest thing I have ever done was beginning the healing process. It was horrible, atrocious, the most heart-wrenching experience I went through, second only to my kids being taken away.

I will not sugarcoat it in the slightest for anyone. I wish someone would have explained to me that it was going to get a whole lot worse before it got better. But I started. I relived all the trauma of my past; both consequences of my own terrible choices and the things that I didn't ask for, put upon me by others. This is when the term codependency was first introduced to me.

Codependency[2]. That word has caused me so much pain in self-reflection. It's hard to be honest about what a train wreck you are. The worst part was that I was on both spectrums as a giver and a taker. My intense need for love and belonging trumped everything in my life. I went through more emotional turmoil learning about codependency than anything else. But

---

2   In codependency, a person tries to satisfy the needs of another who is often controlling or manipulative and who may have an addictive or emotionally unstable personality. "Codependency." Merriam-Webster's Unabridged Dictionary, Merriam-Webster, https://unabridged.merriam-webster.com/unabridged/codependency. Accessed 4 Aug. 2022.

it was also a breath of fresh air. It fit. It explained how I was feeling. I didn't have to try to explain how I was feeling anymore. Owning this word, its definition, and how it affected my life was *the* steppingstone in my journey toward healing.

I made so much progress. I proved to child protective services that I worked hard and was a good mom. My kids were coming home. Then I got sick. I was in full-blown heart failure, and it was challenging the rest of my body. My autonomic nervous system was all over the place, and the stress started affecting my heart and kidneys. Some days I was passed out on the floor more than I was upright. *How could I take care of my kids now?* After a whole lot of hospitalizations and a lifesaving clinical trial, I was on the upswing. My kids came home. Three of them, not four. One of the hardest things I've had to go through is grieving the loss of a child who is still alive. But I stand firm in hope that my prayer, petition, and hard work is eventually realized. That they see the healing that I've done. I hope that I can welcome all my children back home with open arms.

Growth and healing are tough, but so worth the joy you are finally able to feel and exhibit on the flip side of the trials and tribulations that you have to muddle through. The rediscovery of joy allows you to want to be a blessing, and in return to be blessed. It allows you to fill others' cups, and in return have your cup be refilled. Growth doesn't mean that you never have relapses of past parts of your life but that you're able to recover from situations more quickly, own your behavior, reflect on it, and decide how you can do better next time. It allows open communication about strengths and weaknesses with your loved ones. Healing helps foster new relationships that are meaningful.

I have learned that my best and worst personality trait is that I care about others more than myself. I'm still a work in progress when it comes to not letting others affect me. But I'm aware. I'm honest about it. It's getting better, and someday I'm gonna ace this trait!

While I'm working on that, I also realize that one of my best traits is community service. I enjoy teaching veterans and kids how to hunt. In 2020, I found out that my best friend had only one N95 respirator mask to use for over a month, with no idea about when she was going to be issued a new one. That got me pretty fired up. I knew I could gather some materials to make some covers for her mask, but the problem was that I can't sew. So I flooded Facebook groups with my concerns, and I realized my best friend was one of hundreds of thousands in my state in need. We launched a group called the Wisconsin Facemask Warriors. In our area alone, we collected materials and made and distributed 750,000 facemasks for health care workers, first responders, military, and schools within our area.

Even when their effectiveness came into question as the government issued more and more new information, I never could have ended that project. Three people let me know that the warrior project saved their lives because it gave them a purpose during a time that was so unreal. They would have taken their own lives had that project not been around. That's so scary. But the joy those three people and so many others expressed was worth the sixteen- to twenty-hour days in a makeshift distribution center.

There have been plenty of ups and downs along my path. Lots of work to learn to allow myself to have a little grace and self-love. A lot of learning about parenting incredibly different children. But mostly joy when the big stuff is taken care of.

In January of 2021, I became quite ill again and was not able to work. I had to ask for help, and I couldn't quite do things the way that I would like sometimes. I've had to contemplate quality of life and end-of-life choices. I've battled hard both physically and mentally. The best part of this struggle though, is that I recognize my weaknesses, I own the ugly, and because of that I signed my happy butt up for counseling again. It was a bit of a kick in the pants when I made that phone call because it was like I was failing with everything I worked so hard for. But I didn't fail! I was strong enough to ask for help, practicing all the things I learned and needed a refresher on. My counselor helped me to continue to embrace my inner weird and forget chasing the elusive "normal."

I encourage you to take chances, to grow, and to heal. Die with memories, not dreams. Embrace you! Find JOY!

About Liz

LIZ has learned that being imperfectly perfect is the best version of herself. It allows you to embrace your inner weird that makes you, but also allows for growth when needed. She firmly believes growth is an ongoing process throughout life.

Liz's codependency journey and other situations in life nearly made her end it all. But her children were too important to just throw in the towel and give up. Learning self-love helped but learning to give both herself and others some grace in life was a skill that was life changing. Life isn't always easy but finding joy and remembering to search for the little everyday miracles has drastically changed her life.

She is now happily married to an incredible man who is kind, supportive, and has a heart of gold. Liz is a mom and bonus mom to six incredible humans. Daily, she still struggles with physical limitations but her family, the great outdoors, and the skills she has learned help her navigate the hard days better and help her realize how blessed she is on the good days.

Liz says, "You're worthy of experiencing joy. Start healing today! I believe in you!"

CONNECT WITH LIZ

- talktomegoose1015@gmail.com

Sarah Cozzini

DIVORCING ALCOHOL

"I'M DONE," The Fox stated in a stern voice. Sitting across the table, her icy gaze stared me down with seething red hate. I was thrown. The person I trusted to my core and never expected to walk away has said such final words. Within an instant, a snap, I saw nine years of partnership and four years of marriage disappear into darkness. My breath caught. My mind went into survival mode: *How did we get here? How can I stop it? How can I make this rollercoaster from hell rewind? How can I get my person back?* All of this ran through my mind as she stood up and walked away, telling me to go to bed.

Rewind. Reset. Rewind.

As my mind searched for meaning and resolution, I saw flashes of amazing moments flooding me with mental images. Lying under the sun in Hawaii. Christmas with her family making posole. Laughing so hard we could barely breathe. The movie cuddles with our dog, buried in blankets, warm and happy. The passionate sex. *How did we get here?*

Rewind. Then the moments that are harder to admit suddenly surfaced. The trip to Hawaii, littered with continuous alcoholic beverages in between sweet images. The dinners we would make but not eat, as the alcohol took priority. The passionate sex that was a result of too much alcohol consumed that evening. *When was the last time we had sober sex?*

Red flags. A night of alcohol consumption turns from fun to anger to violence quickly. Her hands around my throat, I pushed her back. She threw out her hand, hitting my eye. Blood from a small cut splattered on the wall. Another night of alcohol. A lamp was thrown, cops were called, a domestic violence charge was issued. *Another* night of alcohol ensued into a screaming fight. Phones were thrown, fingers pointed. *Do the bad moments outweigh the good?*

Remembering the multiple attempts and conversations of no longer having alcohol around or in the house. Empty attempts as the following days were surrounded with alcohol. Our work schedules were completely opposite. I would use the time that she wasn't around to drink. My poison was a bottle of wine, a six-pack of Coors Light, and two whiskey shooters. She told me she wouldn't come home because she knew I was drinking. I was not a very nice person when I was drinking, I can admit that. Neither was she. Instead, she would go to the bar with friends and drink, then drive home. Two wrongs don't make a right; that is a definite.

When I first met The Fox, I was twenty years old. She was seeing someone else and continued to see that person for the next five years. The Fox and I formed a friendship over those years, and during those years, I was quite a mess. I went to college and received good grades. I worked as a counselor in the financial aid department. But at night, I was drinking and having one-night stands at every opportunity. Anything to fill the lonely, dark void I had become accustomed to. I got involved in toxic relationships filled with codependency, alcohol, and drug use.

Then, suddenly, The Fox was single. Guess who swooped in to be by her side? I remember kissing her outside a tattoo shop and being surprised when she kissed me back. Her friends told her, "Just have a one-night stand. Sarah is great at that, no strings attached." Well, this time the string attached was my heart. Our one-night stand turned rapidly into an intimate relationship.

Oh, but I am forgetting, I was dating another person at the time. When The Fox asked me to be her girlfriend, I had to leave the room for a second to text the other person I was dating to let them know it "wasn't working out."

So began a nine-year relationship with The Fox. It started out well, as most relationships do. Fun, full of life, hope, and way too much drinking. I think the major turning point was when her father passed away. It was a month before our wedding and the day before my birthday. That's when her aggression started coming out and was directed toward me. Then the resentment started. It was covered up by drunken sex and sweet moments, but it was there. She blamed me for not advancing her career, and I held resentment that she chose her work over me regularly. The spiral continued until those words came out of her mouth. "I'm done."

An interesting thought—when an addiction is present, it feels like you are having an affair. Hang with me here as I try to explain. Imagine a triangle. One corner is you, the other corner is your partner or family or friend, and the third corner is alcohol… or drugs or actually another person. When one or both people have an addiction, it's like that person is having an affair; that addiction becomes a priority. It eclipses the relationship between the two people. So, we were having an affair on one another with alcohol.

Click.

Something went off in my head. I was thirty-three years old, successful in my career as a senior manager for a national company. But my day was: get up, take the dog out, work, drink, go to bed, with her coming in around two a.m. after work. Was that what I really wanted? *No.* That was not what or where I wanted to be in my life at that point.

The first thing that needed to go was the alcohol. I needed to get sober. I found a therapist who specializes in addictions. *Check.* Then I needed to find me. *Who was I? I haven't been alone and single in almost a decade.*

And before that point, I was not a healthy single individual. I'm a different person than I was at twenty-three years old. *So, what do I like?*

That was the toughest part to decipher. *What do I want?*

I needed to find hobbies, so I sprinkled in a little bit of everything I knew to do. Yoga, working out, climbing, and kickboxing. This became my mantra: Therapy. Working out. Yoga. Climbing. Kickboxing. Anytime my career work was done, I needed to do at least one of those things to stay away from the bottle. Gradually, it has become easier. Slowly but surely, the need for that escape, the need to fill a depressed void of being alone lessened.

I began to see the poison that was in my relationship with The Fox. Not only the alcohol, but the way we treated each other. There was love and compassion for each other, but there was something much deeper that we didn't expect to affect us, which took root in grief. Grief of her father passing away, the passing of my grandmother and aunt, grief for the lack of communication. And the need for counseling was ignored.

The hardest parts in a divorce are realizing and accepting the mistakes and recognizing that you cannot control what the other person does or doesn't do in a relationship, as much as you might want to. My relationship with The Fox was not all bad.

I am a stronger individual now. A stronger, more in-tune person than I ever thought I could be. I am still overcoming the cravings for my alcoholic addictions; this is a never-ending work in progress. Getting sober gave me the opportunity to excel further in my career, rekindle friendships I thought were lost, and find my health in hobbies and interests I didn't know existed. And get even stronger.

"Surrender to what is. Let go of what was. Have faith in what will be." —Sonia Ricotti

About Sarah

SARAH COZZINI is a professional in the real estate escrow industry, managing a team for a national company. She was born in Los Angeles in 1988 and moved to Colorado in 1994, where she studied at Metropolitan State University of Denver for a bachelor's degree in Psychology and, later, studied at Colorado State University Global toward a master's degree in Information Technology. She has worn many hats in her professional career, such as financial aid loan counselor, IRA consultant, commercial escrow officer, and manager. Her passion lies in training, as she is avid to teach and learn new processes. She is a huge animal lover of all kinds, kickboxer, yoga enthusiast, paddleboarder, and boulder-climbing hobbyist. Being active brings out the best in her. However, she likes to nerd out with a splatter of video gaming from time to time too.

Emily Mckissick Diaz

BLOODY, BUT UNBOWED

THE FEELING OF THE GENTLE BREEZE flowing through my ponytail, slightly waving it side to side, the smell of the freshly cut grass, and the sun beaming on the tops of my shoulders, turning them a slight shade darker, was the only confirmation I needed to declare that it was all worth it. As I looked down at my soccer cleats covered in red, white, and black, I thought back to the journey I shared with them over the past fifteen years. These musty, worn out, and stern-looking cleats that had traveled with me all over the world, were worth the specialty store price. The beating that these cleats took and how they protected my feet and inspired me to dance as I traveled up and down the field year after year were worth it.

Practice after practice. Win followed by win. Loss followed by even more losses. The insurmountable friendships and teammates I gained within the US and from around the world, was worth it. Traveling from coast to coast in our clunky Suburban to cut costs on hotels and flights was worth it. Traveling to Europe when I was in seventh grade with a handful of teammates hoping to master the game while terribly missing my parents (my number one fans), was worth it. Every closet crying moment, injury, sitting the bench until I earned a starting position, leaving my team after years of playing together to join a new team I thought might help my chances of getting into a Division I school, was worth it. It was all worth it.

And here I was, standing in the middle of a field at one of the most prestigious colleges, to play one of the most respected sports for one of the most competitive Division I schools in the US. I had made it. I made it because I took one goal and I focused on it for fifteen straight years. I spent countless money on trainings, camps, private coaches, tournaments, world travels to more camps, and countless other opportunities. I spent countless time in between studies, dance class, and a small number of fun activities, practicing my craft. Over and over again, until I got it right. My entire adolescence was engulfed by it. I was defined by it. My friends labeled me by it. And I knew with every fiber of my being that I was going to become one of the greatest players to enter the field. I was ready for all that was to join my journey. My mental well-being yearned for it. My family was going to benefit immensely from it. I was going to change the trajectory of the financial blueprint that had haunted my family for way too long. I was going to make it to the top and bless those in the process who weren't as fortunate. It was my job at this point to inspire other women and men of all walks of life to become the best that they could be. And to be honest, I felt like my life's purpose depended on it.

I was in a moment of bliss and pure authenticity. And for the next several months I knew the real work would begin. I would be putting in workouts at 6:00 a.m., followed by several more practices throughout the day. Morning, midmorning, afternoon, and evening, my teammates and I would endure a different type of work ethic. We would partake in drills, long runs, foot work, scrimmages, and so much more. I would work harder than I ever did throughout my middle and high school careers because I wanted that starting position. It was my time to prove to Coach that I was an asset to the team. The distractions of becoming a freshman at a new school were set aside. I knew I didn't have time for all the fun we were intended to participate in as freshmen. This was the time that I had to make sure to finalize my lifelong career. This was the only thing that mattered in my life. And I finally accepted the opportunity to seal my fate.

As I heard Coach yell my name, "Mckissick!" I began to run back toward the sideline and my final thoughts rolled in… I walked onto this team, where I will earn a full ride, I will earn a starting position, and I will earn respect for being a part of a group of individuals who earned the right to play at a Division I school. I was in rarified air. I had made it, it all was worth it, and I was worthy of it.

Or so I thought…

What followed this moment of feeling complete and utter bliss would haunt me for many more years than I care to share.

Without a blink, a complete season under my belt or a full ride to show for it, *I lost it all*. It wasn't the MCL tear I encountered in game six that put me back onto the bench for the rest of the season. It wasn't feeling completely left out of the comradery of the team, nor was it the asinine politics. I lost it all because I didn't realize how fragile I was inside. Up to that point, I thought I had the strength to push through anything. I proved to myself in the past fifteen years that I was stronger than any circumstance life handed to me. My parents raised a young woman who had all the characteristics that qualified her to save the world. But I gave up on her. I walked away from her, and I left her stranded and alone on the field. And I never saw her again.

Why did I give up? Why did I walk away from a full-ride scholarship, a potential lifelong career, and a chance to earn a platform where I could inspire others?

I continuously asked myself this question for twenty years. As I navigated through those twenty years, I tried repeatedly to convince myself that something bigger was on the horizon. And yet I kept hitting a snag. Or rather, a giant boulder that seemed impossible to move. So, when I couldn't move the boulder, I looked for shortcuts. And this ritual and pattern led me down a journey that I call self-sabotage.

At that point in my life, I stayed at the university and continued my studies. I wasn't excited about it, mainly because I felt like I was starting over. There was no Plan B because Plan A was supposed to work out. Starting over felt like what I could imagine losing a child feels like. I would later feel that as well. What I had crafted and molded and designed was gone. Feeling empty and alone, I was spiraling fast. My love for the game and all the feelings it gave me slowly disappeared. I didn't speak to anyone about it because I was ashamed, confused, and embarrassed. I didn't know how to articulate exactly why I gave up. Being so young and still immature, I did what I thought was best at this point. That was to lock myself inside my solo dorm room, study alone, distance myself from new friendships I had made, and figure out my next move. All in complete silence. Away from the noise of the world.

The challenge was that I looked for it in all the wrong places.

As I was healing my knee, I noticed that my continual self-talk was full of animosity and hatred. I had always been a positive expressive person. Growing up, my parents only spoke words of positive praise. It was a loving environment. So, I knew better. But in the next handful of years, it was as if I was entertaining the devil and how he viewed my life. I had become the "con" and the "mark." I suppose it's similar to addiction. Weirdly, it was the only thing I could control in my life.

I would tell myself things like: *No one is going to love you now. You will never fit in with your classmates because you're not that smart or as pretty as the other girls at this school. You came from a working-class family with too many mouths to feed. You will never be enough or have enough. Boys look past you because you don't even know who you are anymore. You are weak.*

These awful affirmations fed my brain for years. And what came of it was evidence to support my claims: awful relationships, mentally, physically, and emotionally. I attracted men who thought the same negative things about me. I sabotaged relationships with my female friends for these men. Thinking I could change how they viewed me, I thought I could make them love me even though I didn't love myself. My lifestyle consisted of parties and sleeping through most of my classes. As an A student who graduated with high honors from high school, I began to receive C and D grades, and finally flunked out of classes. I didn't care. I didn't want any of it anymore.

I was sexually assaulted on campus, and I didn't report it because at that point, I thought I deserved it. And even that I attracted it. Besides, no one is going to care about a failing, worn-out, has-been soccer player who is now barely getting through her classes (and life for that matter).

I did not recognize this girl anymore. I would pray at night for a redo. And yet I woke up time and time again disappointed to see the same train wreck. I could have alerted my parents. They always seemed to have the right answers. But I didn't want to bother them with my issues. They were busy and involved with my siblings' high school careers. It didn't seem fair to me to interrupt all of their happiness. So, I smiled when I needed to and became really good at covering up my wounds when necessary. But at the end of the day when I was at home alone, I would uncover the veil and see all my broken pieces.

And when I thought I couldn't take this pain anymore, a new distraction would arise, and I would partake until again I let that circumstance break me. This was my new pattern. I drank heavily to numb the pain. Thinking my drinking was normal because my classmates were doing it, I later realized they were just numbing their own pain. It was all a chaotic blur.

And then one day, I met the most glorious human. I could write an entire book about the love he and I shared in that moment and for the years that followed. What I didn't realize then was that he was suffering a similar pain. He had also lost it all. He was spiraling, and yet I loved his every imperfection. And let me tell you he treated me like a queen. I had never felt this way around a man other than my father. At first, I thought it was all a ruse just to get me hooked on love. Then the heartbreak would follow. *That's how it works*, I thought. It's what I'd been accustomed to. But he was raised differently. He respected me, and most importantly, he respected himself. Even through his pain. He wasn't jealous; he didn't talk down to me, nor was he ever unfaithful. He looked me in my eyes when he spoke to me, and he actually saw me. All of me.

The moments he and I spent together in the years following, I thought was God's way of telling me I was saved. We spent time traveling and living in Europe with a handful of euros in our pockets. Two twenty-one-year-olds with several battle wounds, exploring the best parts of the world together, hand in hand. It seemed like perfection. But what I found was that my story wasn't over, nor was my growth completed.

My then boyfriend, now husband, and I went through many more years of love, passion, grief, anguish, and more love together. We each carried around our own trauma, chaotically stuffed in a rather beat-up suitcase. Mine was a lot larger in size. We owned it, we named it, and we at times fought hard to keep it. Sometimes I would leave it in the car and other times I would drag it around for everyone else to see. Some thought we were too young to be so committed to one another. But we knew we had found a light within each other that we promised to always keep lit. We had this knowingness about one another that we would never let each other wander alone in the dark.

We have had more happiness and positive moments in our life than strife. However, we both still had a lot of work to do on ourselves. We had a lot of growing to do. Because we both knew with every fiber of our beings that we were put on this earth to help others express the best of themselves. Until we expressed the best for ourselves, our purpose would be unfulfilled.

At this realization, we began our journey of personal development. We read books to gain the tools and resources necessary to continue our growth. We began surrounding ourselves with like-minded individuals who wanted to make a bigger impact in the world. And we finally saw the change within each other and, most importantly, within ourselves.

And then it was as if the Universe didn't think we had learned the lesson quite like she intended. On the evening of April 25, 2010, we encountered one of the most terrifying nights of my life. Matt and I decided to head back to Denver after a long night of dancing at a friend's wedding. It was getting late, and I needed to be at work at 7:00 a.m., so we started our journey back toward home. After being in the car for what seemed like a few moments, an animal-like figure was lying in the middle of the road. Matt swerved the car to miss it, and we collided into a semitruck that was going in the same direction. As my head smacked against the side of the window, the car bounced off of the semitruck and swerved right into the ditch. We continued for several hundred feet as the car took out the fencing in the center of the ditch. To my luck, my seat was laid down and the fence wire brushed quickly above me. My first thought was that this is how people die in car accidents. My second thought was that Matt's seat was sitting straight up and he wasn't that lucky. My third thought was that I didn't want to die this way—my work on earth wasn't completed yet. And then everything went silent and dark.

We survived the car wreck, but not as we had been before. We had simultaneously transcended from our current beings to something bigger and greater. It is difficult to put this feeling into words. What I know is that from that evening forward, I began to let go of those boulders weighing down my suitcase. I saw how my life could be full of abundance, happiness, strength, and grace. And I felt as I once did in my adolescence. I saw love again. At the end of the day, I felt too blessed to be stressed.

Although I saw the car wreck as a symbol, I promised to live my life seeking and fulfilling my life's work. Knowing those boulders that continue to lie in my path may still be big and mighty, my strength was showing up differently. I found better solutions to move those boulders out of my path. And I began a new way of looking at my life. I would be remiss to say that I did all of this on my own. I did have the support and help from family, friends, and my husband. Especially when I allowed them back into my life and my heart. I found the beauty and courage within to be vulnerable. And I also found that sharing my story inspired others to do the same.

I am incredibly grateful for the opportunities that have afforded my growth. I am elated to have discovered that I never lost that girl. She was always with me, supporting me and loving me through it all.

INVICTUS

Out of the night that covers me,
Black as the Pit from pole to pole,
I thank whatever gods may be
For my unconquerable soul.
In the fell clutch of circumstance
I have not winced nor cried aloud.
Under the bludgeonings of chance
My head is bloody, but unbowed.
Beyond this place of wrath and tears
Looms but the horror of the shade,
And yet the menace of the years
Finds, and shall find, me unafraid.
It matters not how strait the gate,
How charged with punishments the scroll,
I am the master of my fate:
I am the captain of my soul.

—*William Earnest Henley*

About Emily

EMILY MCKISSICK DIAZ was born and raised in Colorado. For over twenty-one years, Emily and her husband Matt have resided in Denver, Colorado, where they both attended college. Emily lived in Granada and Valencia Spain, studying Spanish and multicultural education, and later completed her bachelor's and master's degrees from the University of Denver and went on to pursue a life as an entrepreneur.

In 2005, Emily partnered with a company, PPLSI, where she marketed legal and identity theft services and built a team of associates across the US. She and her husband worked with the company for over a decade. They both trained and educated numerous associates and teams on how to grow their book of business.

Emily worked several different jobs and careers throughout the years in order to fulfill her responsibilities while creating and building her business. In 2018, she launched her personal growth company.

Emily sits on the Board of Directors for Lardon (an adult day program for those who have intellectual and developmental disabilities). She is also the CEO and Founder of Enlightened Warrior Book Club, a book club that inspires you to be the best expression of yourself, one book at a time.

CONNECT WITH EMILY

- EnlightenedWarriorBookClub.com

Sydney Jackson-Clockston

UPROOTING NEGATIVE SELF-TALK

AS I WRITE THIS, my hands still tremble with anxiety. Here I am, a thirty-year-old quaking at a childhood memory of the monsters that hurt me and my family. At six years old, I learned that the monsters to be afraid of are not imaginary ones hiding in a dark closet or under your bed. Oh no. Some monsters are very much real, made of flesh and bone, that have a way of leaving an imprint on your life. I'll never forget what it felt like to learn, in a moment of violence, that society was not built for me and that monsters are real. I remember the pounding on my grandmother's living room door. I remember the group of men bursting through after my mom cracked it open. I remember the commotion, the yelling, the guns. I remember my grandmother blacking out while her face was being squashed into the couch as a man pinned her down with his knee on her upper back and neck. I remember my mother's cry as she lay on the ground, seven months pregnant, in restraints. I remember the twisted look of hate on their faces. I remember the men yelling, "Get these niggers out of here!" I remember the feeling as an adult, finding out that the ringleader said he would have shot the "little nigger" (referring to me), but he couldn't think of a good enough explanation to justify the action. I remember the men's uniforms and their badges. I will always remember my first interaction with the police.

Spring 1997: My mom and I went to the grocery store with my grandmother. We got back to her place to see a dog catcher sitting outside of the house. She accosted my mom and grandmother, yelling that the dog had gotten out of the yard. We could see through the chain-link fence on the side of the house that Muffin, my mom's childhood dog, was in the backyard right where he should be. My grandmother had diabetes, and while we were out her blood sugar had gotten low. My mom helped my grandmother into the house and continued to unload the groceries. Mom dismissed the dog catcher, who was visibly furious, and the dog catcher threatened to call the police on my mom and grandmother.

My mom and grandmother both ended up trapped in jail over the weekend for processing, and I spent the weekend worried about them. I was also upset that Muffin had been removed and expeditiously euthanized by the city pound. Unbeknownst to me, my mom and grandmother had a long legal road ahead of them. The only reason they did not spend more time in jail and get convicted of aggravated battery of police officers is because a rookie cop stood up and told the truth. He shared that he joined law enforcement to help people and not harm and abuse them and falsify reports. His account of events matched up with my mom's and grandmother's story. The judge told my mom that she and my grandmother were lucky the rookie spoke up or they would have both faced jail time. And yes, this group of officers was allowed to stay on the force and continue to abuse and terrorize others. Not too long after this experience, my mother started having conversations with me about womanhood and safety in our society. She also had to impart knowledge on how to survive our society as a Black woman, including interactions with the police. In Black culture, it is called "The Talk." The Talk was a conversation intended to mitigate potential harm from taking place against my Black body.

COMMON ITEMS COVERED IN THE TALK

Always carry a receipt in your hand when you leave the store and hold it visibly. When you're in a store, don't carry items around the store unless they are in a basket.

You are Black and a woman. Expect to work ten times harder to make it half as far. Exceptionalism is a must in order to be tolerated and experience any sort of growth professionally.

If you're pulled over by the police, make sure to stop on a busy road where other people can see what's going on. Be courteous and calm even in an emergency situation.

Never let them see you cry. *Never* let them (white folks) see you cry.

The Talk was imperative to my survival. I live in a world that was not systematically created for me to thrive. Between The Talk and my actual lived experience, it was reinforced in my head that any day could really and truly be my last.

Spring 2019: I was working remotely from home for a regional cooperative, hired to coordinate trainings, plan philanthropic events, organize monthly board meetings, and make sales for additional commission. I was miserable. My boss micromanaged me more and more. In the organization, I was the youngest person, one of the only women, and the *only* Black, Indigenous, People of Color (BIPOC) person. Emotionally, I was mean to my family. Mentally, I was exhausted. And physically, my health was declining. I was sick and tired of being sick and tired.

Something just snapped inside of me. It might have been during the board meeting where they (the Board) were upset that the minimum wage was going up, all the while complaining about low employee retention. Perhaps it was that our philanthropy work (one of the only things I really enjoyed about that damn job) was always a contest. Instead of folks giving out of the kindness of their hearts, everything was gamified. Or maybe it was when our nonprofit partner really needed our volunteer support at an event, and only two people managed to make it. Or maybe it was the time my boss berated me because the catering was late for an event. Or maybe it was the fact that I kept being handed secretarial tasks, something I was not hired for. Those tasks prevented me from making my own sales calls while giving my boss the time and freedom to increase her sales. Or it could have been the time my boss emailed me, explaining how unprofessional my written communications were because of my dyslexia, while making several typos and grammatical errors herself…

Whatever it was, I was sick of the bullshit. I had always wanted to start my own business. My mom and my partner both kept encouraging me to. My self-talk, on the other hand, was out of control, saying things like:

- You can't spell. Who the hell is going to trust you with their business?
- You're not an expert! Who would pay to listen to you?
- You're fat. People don't listen to fat people.
- You're Black, living in Colorado. No one is going to see your value.

While I was still working for the cooperative, I took a small step forward by pushing down all the negative self-talk swirling in my head and starting my own side hustle. Mind you, I had tried many side hustles while working for this organization, but this was the first that I could say was my own business. One day, my boss pulled me to the side and said that she was concerned that the side business was affecting my work. Maybe the position I was in was "no longer a good fit." Talk about gaslighting![3] Now that I think about it, I believe this conversation was my breaking point. I was tired of working my ass off for others who did not see my value, and I was tired of having low self-worth.

I wrote my resignation letter. I drafted the email and sat on it for a few days. After talking with my partner and having his support, I grabbed a glass of wine, took a deep breath, and pressed the send button. So now what? I knew my mindset was fucked. Since I was six years old, I had spent my whole life in fear of what had happened and what might happen to me. I knew that if I was going to be what I considered to be successful, I was going to have to work my damn hardest to unlearn negative self-talk and relearn self-worth, self-compassion, and healthy boundaries. While working to grow my business I took on a couple of gigs working for Lyft and Instacart. These jobs allowed me the time, freedom, and cash to pay my bills. I also decided to invest in myself, doing my own self-investment audit to see how much I was really taking care of myself. I looked at my health, finances, work, relationships, self-care, personal growth, and professional growth. By doing this, I discovered that eighty-five percent of my attention had been going to my work. It was shocking to see the truth on paper. My life was devoted to something I hated, and my negative self-talk acted as blinders.

It's funny how the universe works. I was attending a networking meeting when I bumped into a guy who had started his own coaching firm. He saw something in me that no stranger had ever been bold enough to share. He

---

3   Psychological manipulation of a person usually over an extended period of time that causes the victim to question the validity of their own thoughts, perception of reality, or memories and typically leads to confusion, loss of confidence and self-esteem, uncertainty of one's emotional or mental stability, and a dependency on the perpetrator. *Merriam-Webster's Unabridged Dictionary*, Merriam-Webster, accessed July 22, 2022. https://unabridged.merriam-webster.com/collegiate/gaslighting.

said that I was a powerful force and that I was dimming my light to make others comfortable. I had to sit with that for a few days, but I eventually concluded that he was right. While I didn't have funds at the time to pay for coaching, he was extremely understanding and offered to coach me if I helped him with event creation and management. It was a no-brainer. Investing in coaching was the second biggest thing I had done that year next to quitting my job. I had a guide to support me in answering some really difficult, self-reflective questions:

- What kind of life would I like to have?
- What are my values?
- What am I passionate about?
- What's my legacy?
- What are my gifts?

And how can I use them to build up a business and the community at the same time?

In addition to coaching, I was able to build a community with his other clients who were on a similar journey personally and professionally. This was the first time in my life that I built relationships with shared values and folks were doing the same for me.

I started experiencing clarity beyond my wildest dreams, which, in itself, is a form of freedom. I now know that I have struggled with imposter syndrome. My imposter syndrome stems from a combination of lived experiences like surviving police brutality, having a few shitty bosses, and having a stepfather who was a narcissist, compounded with my own negative self-talk. I also now know how to catch myself when I start to travel down the imposter syndrome rabbit hole of low self-worth and perfectionism.

Spring 2022: My eyes and mind are now open. I have an amazing network of folks that I can reach out to, including my therapist, previous coach, family, and friends. My wildest dreams are coming true. I am now a published author despite my dyslexia. I have a successful coaching practice. I gave a paid workshop with my alma mater for 200 graduating seniors and alumni. I was the host of a virtual international conference with 600 attendees. I host life-changing retreats and events. Most importantly, I trust that no matter what life throws at me, I will not only survive but thrive.

We all have unique lived experiences that involve surviving monsters at some point. When you have an encounter with monsters, their actions likely leave a negative impact, adding to and reinforcing negative self-talk. I offer up several questions that you can start thinking about in relation to your own life. Slow down and spend fifteen to twenty minutes reflecting on these questions before you turn the page. I want to leave you with the simple but powerful tool of reframing negative self-talk. It's time to flip the script:

Negative: No one cares what I have to say.
Reframe: My lived experience has value, and what I have to say matters.

Negative: I haven't reached my goals fast enough.
Reframe: I'm moving at the exact right pace for me. It is not a competition.

Negative: I need to be perfect.
Reframe: Who benefits from me pretending to have it all together when I don't? What support do I need right now? If no one can give me the support I desire, how can I give it to myself?

Negative: I am fat.
Reframe: I am grateful for my body and for all that it allows me to do.

Whatever the negative thought is in your head, *stop and reframe it*. You got this! And remember, *passion* over perfection.

About Sydney

SYDNEY JACKSON-CLOCKSTON is the owner and founder of Citrine Unlimited LLC, a multifaceted organization that provides coaching, training, public speaking, and retreat design. Sydney's mission is to use Citrine Unlimited LLC as a tool of empowerment and transformation for its clients.

Sydney is invested in making a positive impact on her community. She works part time as an entrepreneurial training specialist and coach with Rocky Mountain MicroFinance Institute. Sydney is a holistic wellness advocate for individuals with neurodiversities and physical disabilities. She sits as a board member with Guided By Humanity (GBH). Sydney also enjoys volunteering with youth and offers leadership development through Colorado Young Leaders (CYL).

CONNECT WITH SYDNEY

- Website: citrineunlimited.com
- LinkedIn: sydneyjc
- Instagram: citrineunlimited
- linktr.ee/CitrineUnlimited

Janet Langmeier

YOU COMPLETE ME

AS A WOMAN WHO HAS BEEN married and divorced three times, "you complete me" was practically a mantra from the time I was a little girl. Raised in a time when home economics classes literally taught "Tips to Look after Your Husband" as a central part of the curriculum, looking for someone to complete me seemed to be my predestined goal in life. I did not know it then but looking for someone or something to complete me would dominate decades of my life.

The oldest of eight, I grew up taking care of my younger sisters and brothers, helping with housework and chores. Despite the long list of tasks, we had a lot of fun—after the work was done.

School was a different story. I loved learning, but I hated school. The principal of our school was a nun who used meanness as a natural extension of her discipline. I clearly remember her telling me throughout my school days how dumb and insignificant I was, and that no one would marry me or find me attractive. Imagine how disconcerting that was to my predestined goal of finding a man to complete me! Not only did her words confuse and hurt me, but the ongoing message of unworthiness was a lot for a five-year-old to take in and hear repeated for the next seven years. I was not singled out for this kind of treatment; the sister was generous in her condemnation of the children in her charge. Many a young one from those years has even sadder tales to tell. I count myself among the lucky from her classroom reign.

I married for the first time when I was a naive girl of eighteen. Not understanding the difference between sex and love, I thought I was in love with my boyfriend. The warning signals were there, but in my youth and inexperience I did not recognize them. I was looking for my completion, my other half. A good Catholic girl must be in love if she is having sex with her boyfriend, so I convinced myself I was in love. I married the poor boy and had four children with him. I spent all fourteen years of my marriage to him seeking that sense of completion. All the years we spent together were not awful. We had good times, and my children have always been my greatest joy. However, I felt empty in the marriage while trying to find fulfillment and satisfaction in my job and as a mom. I felt as though I failed miserably at all of it. Starving for the experience of completion, I finally divorced him.

When I met my second husband, I was desperately lonely, broke, homeless, and insecure, with four kids from ages one to eleven. My second husband was charming and a lot of fun. He swept me off my feet. I was so starstruck, and certain of my completion in this relationship, that I did not see any of the raging red flags waving in my face.

My first husband had a foul temper. I was often despondent about it, believing that if I could keep him happy, he would not get mad so often. He turned out to be a minor league player in temper compared to husband number two. A recovering alcoholic, my second husband suffered wild mood swings. We did not know who or what we would be coming home to from one day to the next. Although he did not drink during our fourteen-year marriage, his mood swings were savage! No one in our home was safe, and everyone ran for cover when he was in a bad temper. I came to understand what walking on eggshells really meant. It is a wonder and a blessing to me that my children have forgiven me for that marriage. When things were good, they were immensely good… only to be followed by vastly, bad. I spent those years blaming myself, wondering what was wrong with me, trying to make peace, and protect everyone. It was an exhausting existence.

At my parent's fortieth wedding anniversary celebration, he physically hit me for the first time. We were in Wisconsin, where I did not have any money or a car, so I felt trapped, with no other option but to go back home to Colorado. In hindsight, refusing to return to Colorado with him would have been wiser, but I did not want my parents to know I was failing yet again as a wife and mother. I am embarrassed to admit that it took another physical threat to my person before I took action to get out of the marriage. By this time, my oldest son had moved out on his own, and my oldest daughter was married, with a husband and daughter of her own. My youngest daughter, for a brief time, sought refuge in a relationship that turned out to be abusive. She had the courage to leave the situation quickly. My youngest son briefly escaped into drugs. I was past feeling that I was failing miserably. I knew I was failing miserably, on many fronts.

My children rallied together to help me recover. For a period, they all came home to live with me, giving us a chance to heal together. I am forever grateful to my children for that gift. That time together gave my oldest daughter and her husband an opportunity to save up a down payment for their first home. My youngest daughter found a good job and met her future husband. My sons stayed with me a little longer until they moved into an apartment that they shared. By this time my youngest son, having left drugs behind, was in college.

My search for completion was not yet over, when years later I met my last husband. We worked together, and I thought I knew him well from seeing his day-to-day interactions with clients. During this marriage, all the years of not taking care of myself, not listening to my inner voice, and not understanding what I was really looking for in terms of completion, came crashing down around me. My physical health was at the lowest of my life, my emotional health was stretched to the limit, and my mental health was threadbare.

My caretaker personality was in full swing once again. I had married a man with serious mental health issues. After ten years of taking care of him, it became clear he needed more than I could provide on my own. On the advice of his physicians, he and I planned together to get him the help he needed while taking pressure off me. We legally separated. I bought him an apartment, furnished it, and moved him in. For a long time, I helped him manage his finances, pay his bills, and take care of apartment maintenance. He became unhappy with the arrangement and wanted to divorce. I agreed, and we amicably divorced, using the separation we had agreed upon years earlier. A few years after that, he sued me for divorce. His attorney was shocked to find out that we had been legally divorced for several years already. Such was his mental state by that time.

One would think I would finally be learning my lesson. I did have enough insight to realize that the common denominator in all three of my marriages was me. I understood that if anything was to change, it had to be me. I had to look at this notion of seeking completion in someone or something else.

At first, the freedom of being single was exhilarating. For the first time in my life, I felt truly free. Unfortunately, my health had deteriorated. All the years of stress had taken a toll, and having suffered diverticulitis for years, I finally underwent colon surgery. Given a clean bill of health, a new life as a single woman lay ahead of me.

Now the real work of completion began. Always interested in spirituality, philosophy, and personal development, I started taking classes and reading books. I joined a women's a cappella competitive chorus and brought singing back into my life, lost considerable weight, and felt good about the future.

That is when the real test came! A man I had known for twenty years reached out to me after his wife died. We had always been good friends, and I had introduced him to his wife. We started seeing each other and we were enjoying one another's company. Then he wanted to change our friendship to a romance. I thought, "Finally, a man I have known, loved, and trusted for twenty years. This is the completion I have always looked for." Let's just say that no matter how long you have known someone, until you are in a relationship, you only see fragments. Here I was continuing to attract another unhealthy, unhappy, unfulfilling relationship. We managed to part friends, although I hit my bottom in ways that left me unsure of myself and my continued existence on the planet. I was mired in an abyss that felt beyond my capacity to free myself from. It was one of the lowest passages of my life.

Fortunately, I did have the capacity to free myself. All my study and a new appreciation of myself came into play. I also have amazing children, and my beautiful family was there for me. I took time off from work, connected with a friend who is a mental health professional for guidance, and began the journey into myself, which became the groundwork for the *badass* woman I feel I am today.

I then asked myself a whole new set of questions. Instead of, *How do I find someone to complete me, or how do I make someone happy?* I asked myself, *What gives me more life? What would I love?*

The answers to those questions took me down a completely new path. I began deeper studies of spirituality, neuroscience, health, and nutrition, which led me to earn my Health Coach Certification. I also completed studies to become a Certified Dream Builder® Coach and Life Mastery™ Consultant. I started my transformational life coaching practice in 2017. Since then, I have had the honor and privilege to coach amazing women and men, helping them achieve their dreams. Plus, I have co-authored three books, started teaching workshops, and even became a certified TranscenDance™ facilitator, which fulfilled my secret lifelong dream to dance! My deeply held desire to lead transformational retreats is also coming true as my first Joy Lift Transformational Retreat is on the books!

I am so happy and grateful for the life I am living today. This mother's dream for her children is for them to be happy. I am thrilled that all four of my children are happy and in great places in their lives.

What cracks us open only helps us grow if we are willing to take a good look at ourselves and acknowledge that we are worthy of living a life we love. I now know that the completion I looked for in others is, and has always been, within me. Being at peace and at one with the power that breathes me is what gives me life, supports my dreams, and emboldens me to encourage others.

When I look in the mirror today, I say to myself, "You complete me," and I know it is true!

About Janet

FOR FORTY-PLUS YEARS, Janet Langmeier has been a dedicated spiritual explorer, studying transformational principles. A Certified Dream Builder Coach® and Life Mastery™ Consultant, Infinite Possibilities Trainer, and TranscenDance™ Facilitator, Janet blends spiritual principles with practical, real-world application in her coaching and teaching.

Throughout her career, Janet has helped people successfully transform their lives in the areas of career, education, relationships, spirituality, body image, and health. No stranger to the work of transformation, Janet's ongoing journey to full-spectrum, abundant living is the driving passion behind her desire to coach and help others. Janet's workshops, coaching programs, and retreats help people break through limitations and achieve greater results than they've known before.

Co-author of *Short, Sweet & Sacred: Uplifting Stories from Life Coaches Who Overcame and Moved from Stuck to Success*, *Hold My Crown: Women of Grit Share Stories of Resilience*, and coming soon, *Happiness Matters*.

CONNECT WITH JANET

- Website: phoenixsoaringintl.com
- Facebook: phoenixsoaringintl
- Instagram: phoenixsoaringintl
- LinkedIn: janet-langmeier-51337293

Coral Laski

GETTING OUT OF MY OWN WAY

"Our deepest fear is not that we are inadequate. Our deepest fear is that we are powerful beyond measure. It is our light, not our darkness, that most frightens us… as we let our own light shine, we unconsciously give other people permission to do the same. As we're liberated from our own fear, our presence automatically liberates others."
—Marianne Williamson

WHAT DOES IT MEAN TO BE A BADASS? To me, it's "**B**roken **a**nd **D**efeated, but **A**lways **S**tay **S**miling."

I've been a victim as well as a perpetrator of pain. We are all victims of other victims because hurt people hurt people. I've experienced abuse physically, mentally, and verbally. I've been taken advantage of sexually and allowed others to hurt me. These things are all true, but the biggest abuser in my life was me to myself. Today, I am strong, confident, and believe that I have unlimited power and grace within me to succeed in life. It was not a short or smooth road that I traveled to get to this point. However, somewhere deep inside was this person all along. No matter how far we travel in the wrong direction, there's always a chance to reroute.

Too often, we let our past mistakes and pain define our present and our future. It is not a safe place for me to dwell in the past, but it is important to remember and use those experiences as fuel to create a better present. I survived my past and am here to write this story today.

As a young girl growing up in Louisiana, my parents moved me from the public school system into a private Catholic school, in fourth grade. At the time, I remember feeling like the only new kid and did not fit in with anyone. I was there for just a year before my family moved to Colorado. It was summer when we moved, so it wasn't easy to meet friends before school started. Coming from a very different climate, there was a bit of a learning curve in how to dress. I was a sporty girl and followed the lead of my brother by wearing baggy pants or gym clothes most of the time. I also had a deep southern accent, which led to me receiving some help with phonics and pronunciation in school.

My middle school years were relatively uneventful, but there were a few moments that I think of as turning points. I once stood up for a boy being teased in band class, and the bully pushed me into the teacher's podium, ultimately breaking one wrist and spraining the other. The physical injuries were just the beginning of the emotional pain I would inflict upon myself. To this day, confrontation is a struggle of mine. *Could it stem from the embarrassment or pain that I felt that day?*

Kids can be cruel and say very hurtful things. Why do people say that "sticks and stones may break my bones, but words will never hurt me?" I think that is a downright lie.

Broken bones heal.

Painful words burn into painful memories.

Other people put labels on me before I even understood the meaning behind them; "awkward, different, crazy, loud …" Labels have a way of sticking with us over time, and in many ways, I started to embody them in my beliefs and my actions. The one that persisted through time was this nagging idea that I wasn't good enough, no matter what I looked like, wore, did, said, or accomplished.

During my first year of high school, I got very sick. The doctors couldn't figure out what was wrong, and I was in constant pain. Colonoscopy, biopsy, ultrasound, probes—I don't know how many tests and procedures I went through to determine the cause of my pain.

Eventually, I tested positive for mononucleosis, but instead of attacking my spleen, it went after my liver and gallbladder. My best friend (also fourteen years old) was the first to notice the yellow tint in my skin and looked in her dad's medical books to determine I was jaundiced, and something was wrong with my liver. I presented this information to my doctor, who blew me off because my friend was "just a kid" and I was too young to have anything wrong with my liver. Come to find out, my gallbladder had nearly shut down because of the stones that had grown within it.

The solution was to have a major surgery, removing my gallbladder, appendix, and a piece of my liver. The surgery was scheduled for July of the same summer that my family moved to another new city. My brothers went to stay at our grandparents' house in Iowa, and they left me alone at home, in a new town, for over a month before the surgery. All my friends were over an hour away. Because I was so sick, I couldn't meet any of my neighbors or new schoolmates.

After healing from the surgery, I was never more excited in my life to go back to school! I entered my sophomore year as one of about fifty new students and felt like I just got lost in the mix. I was so lonely and eager to make friends that I latched on to the first people who would hang out with me. Many of them were labeled as the troublemakers, but I didn't care, I just wanted to feel accepted. I prided myself on being a good student who valued my education and schoolwork. But I stopped doing my best for a while because my friends thought it was uncool.

In fact, in hindsight, I have spent a great deal of my life trying to please others or be whoever I thought I needed to be for them to like me. I also have a caregiving nature, and my mother likes to tell me that I gravitate toward those I believe I can help or lift up in some way. Perhaps this is the reason being a teacher and a mother is my calling in life.

College was an exciting whirlwind of experiences and lessons. Most of the struggles and pain I went through were self-inflicted. I loved to party and could outlast some of the best! One of my best friends and I used to refer to ourselves as "Sinful Angels," getting in trouble occasionally but still performing our best in school. I finished with two degrees and a 3.7 GPA overall, getting accepted directly into graduate school.

Once I turned 21, I started drinking alcohol heavily, especially on the weekends. I didn't think anything was wrong with this because everyone I hung out with was doing the same thing. I drank to celebrate, to connect, to escape, to numb, and to hide the feelings or shyness I felt within. At some point, I found myself sporadically blacking out, where I couldn't remember the details of what happened the night before. My friends and I thought we were slick, coming up with creative ways to drive around, selecting someone as the "designated less-drunk driver." This is a scary thing to think about now, but fortunately God was on our side, and we never hurt ourselves or anyone else.

One night, I decided to leave a party to drive home, but I made a wrong turn and ended up on a cul-de-sac and hit a tree. In my stupor, I believed my friends just left me in my crashed car and went to a party, so I decided it was a good idea to blast my horn until they came back. They never showed up, but some lovely police officers did. It's written in my report that I thanked them for coming to get me, because "I shouldn't be driving right now." I also sang my alphabet backwards, a fun trick I can do that I used to joke would get me out of a DUI. It didn't.

Luckily, they let my mom come pick me up, and I never spent any time in jail. I went through the classes and process that was necessary for the courts and DMV. When they tell you to take a cab, it's well worth it. I easily spent over $15,000 throughout the course of this experience. To this day, I thank God for the way that night ended, and that the only thing I hurt was the headlight on my car.

In the therapy classes, they treated everyone with a DUI as an alcoholic, which I resented. I had only been drinking for less than a year, so how could I be an alcoholic. "Those kinds of people are nasty, or homeless, or crazy... I'm just a normal twenty-one-year-old." Retrospectively, I am thankful for that experience, because later in life, when I really wanted help, I knew where to turn.

I finished graduate school at the top of my class, with a 4.0 GPA, yet I drove around with an Interlock machine in my car (*a breathalyzer connected to the car's ignition*). Bring on some feelings of unworthiness or less-than mentality. I even began my professional career at my university with that lovely contraption in my car. It was five years all together before I was able to get it taken off, and I will never have it again.

Very few people in my life knew about the extent to which alcohol flooded my life. I worked an eight to five job, was professional and respected, but nearly drowned myself to sleep at night. The pain within, plus the inability to stop my mind from racing, was a real struggle. I used to think I was totally crazy and unique in this experience, which made me spiral out of control even more. No matter how much success I gained, accomplishments I earned, or accolades I received, I believed I wasn't good enough. I don't know where this idea came from, or why I treated myself so poorly as a result. Even getting in trouble with the law, I felt like an outcast because I wasn't bad enough to be a "real criminal."

I used to tell myself that I had to experience tough times and suffer through my addictive personality so that I could one day help others. I knew deep down that I would find the strength one day to overcome the pain, learn healthy habits, and feel confident and content as I am.

A few years after graduate school, I had my first child, my son. He is my angel, my love, and he transformed my life. The day I found out I was pregnant, I instantly stopped drinking to protect my baby. About two years later, I was pregnant with my daughter; my princess and my blessing. I was fortunately able to breastfeed both of my babies. I nursed my son throughout my pregnancy and tandem nursed them for about a year before I weaned him. A year later, I weaned her because I was getting ready to go on a trip for a week. Ultimately, I ended up nursing for about five years. As difficult as it is to admit, one of the reasons I chose to breastfeed so long was because it kept me away from drinking. However, once I stopped nursing, I went on an all-inclusive trip to Jamaica, and my love for drinking was reignited.

For the next year and a half, I battled on and off with alcohol. I was divorced, living as a single mother in my dad's house, no longer working at the university, and struggling with my identity. I felt that my life was over before it even really began. In March 2020, COVID hit our world and put us into a lockdown. Suddenly, I couldn't go anywhere. One of the few places that remained open was the liquor store. I found myself drinking earlier and earlier; heavier and heavier. Four months of this and I was in shambles. I couldn't look at myself in the mirror; I despised who I had become. I pride myself on being an active and present mother, so that remained a priority to me throughout this time, but I felt like I was killing myself from the inside out. One day it hit me—I can't do this to myself—my babies need me. Sure, my babies had plenty of family around to support them, but I am the only person who will ever love them as much as I do. I needed to change for myself and for them.

It's funny how I can find a reason to feel not good enough no matter what situation I am in. Even in my darkest moments, I convinced myself that I wasn't good enough for help because my issues weren't "bad enough" compared to others.

How did I become this person? What's wrong with me? Who am I really? What do I want in life? How can I love myself? Those were the questions on my mind the day I walked into my first recovery meeting. My cousin brought me to the most amazing group of people I have ever met in my life. I expected to enter a dark room with a bunch of miserable sober people talking about how much they hated life.

Instead, I found laughter, companionship, strength, and encouragement. I instantly felt that I wanted that for myself. If they could do it, so could I. I have never been a part of something so open, honest, and reflective in my life. The stories, raw emotions, and vulnerability I heard and saw from others changed my life.

It started with the belief that I am worthy. I am good enough. I deserve happiness.

One thing that I have found most fascinating is how many exceptional, amazing, successful, strong, beautiful, and kind people grace the world of recovery. I don't know a single family that isn't affected by addiction or abuse in some way. The stigma surrounding addiction and alcoholism needs to be smashed. As a society, we are bombarded daily with ads for liquor or beer, as well as ads for pharmaceutical drugs. Doctors prescribed unnecessary medications all the time, often bringing a "normal" person past the point of no return and into a spiraling addiction.

There is beauty in recovery and so much joy to be had in life. There will be difficult times, that's a given, but learning to work through my emotions has been the most freeing experience in the world. For the first time in my life, I chose to do something that was one hundred percent for me. My children, family, friendships, and future relationships all benefit from that decision. However, I was the only person who could make the change.

I used to feel lonely in a crowded room of people, but I now feel connected and loved, even when I'm alone. One of the most unexpected yet exciting outcomes of this journey is my newfound ability to be alone with myself and be happy. When you are content and feel joy being alone, you tend to allow only those who will uplift you further into your life.

If you are struggling with the same feelings of unworthiness or feel depressed and defeated, I know there is hope for you too. I told myself for years to smile, put on a happy face, and persevere. Today, I smile genuinely because I am positive and proud of who I am and where I am going. I've wasted too much time worrying about what others think, embarrassed by what they would say if they knew the truth about me and my past. Writing this story is helping me move past that fear and inspire others to no longer allow shame from their past to impact their present.

We all have a past, most of us must do some dumb things, learn the hard way, and grow from the experience. It is in sharing our stories, honestly and humbly, that we can heal the pain in the world.

Here are some tidbits I've learned along the way that have immensely helped me shape my mindset into becoming the woman I am today:

- Today is the tomorrow that I was so worried about yesterday. So, if I'm able to wake up in the morning, why let the troubles from yesterday steal my chance for joy today?
- If you can't do anything about it, then it isn't really a problem. It just is what it is.
- Don't blame anyone else in life. Good people bring happiness, bad people give experience, worse people provide a lesson, and the best people deliver memories.
- What other people think of me is none of my business.
- My ego says, "I'll find peace when everything falls into place." God tells me, "Everything will fall into place when I find peace."

The biggest lesson I've learned is this: I am my own worst enemy; I stand in my own way more than anyone else. When I'm stressing, worrying, or overthinking everything wrong that I could have done or said, other people are likely not even concerned with me. They're generally focusing on their own issues and behaviors.

You determine your own happiness in life. We are all uniquely and divinely created, with amazing talents to share with the world. I would love to see more encouragement and less ridicule. More inspiration and less criticism. More empowerment and less discrimination. More love and less hate. The world would be a much better place if we all just **S**incerely **M**ove **I**n **L**ove **E**veryday (SMILE).

About Coral

CORAL LASKI is a firm believer in lifelong learning. Her favorite saying is "to teach once is to learn twice." Her passion in life is helping others succeed and find their authentic voice. Every one of us has a talent to share with the world. It's time to find yours.

Earning her bachelor's degrees in both psychology and communication (with an emphasis in leadership studies), as well as a master's degree in communication studies, set her on the path of teaching in higher education. Coral currently teaches at the university and community college in her hometown. Every semester, she learns from the experiences and knowledge of her students, while providing them with valuable tools they can apply in their own lives.

She also owns her own business, Your Best Self Consulting (YBS), where she brings her enthusiasm and expertise to members of her community. She is active in her community, serving on multiple committees and at her children's school through the PTO.

She is a mother to two amazing children, her son and daughter. They enjoy spending time together and share a love of books, pajama dance parties, trips to the zoo, lots of snuggling time.

CONNECT WITH CORAL

- Website: ybsconsulting.com
- Facebook: YourBestSelfConsulting
- Instagram: Coral.Laski
- LinkedIn: Coral Laski

Caroline Lemieux

UNFUCKWITHABLE

"Pain will leave once it is done teaching you."
—attributed to Bruce Lee

WHEN I LOOK AT MYSELF IN THE MIRROR, all that I AM—a ray of sunshine, bold, and becoming grander each day, I can't believe I have been through hell and back, surviving the darkest nights, hiding the knives, drowning, and ashamed to ask for help.

But I did go through it all and I did *survive*, with the crazy chaos I felt within myself, I AM stronger than ever, ready to share my journey; my imperfect story of struggles that have shaped me the way I AM today.

I love this quote and I think it describes perfectly how my life unfolded: "The greater your storm, the brighter your rainbow."

June 2011: "Ready to go home, Miss Lemieux?" asked the hospital nurse, three days after being admitted for my emergency C-section.

No way am I ready to go home, I thought. Home is an hour away. I am tired, hurting, and just the idea of going home was already overwhelming. Just the thought of all the daily chores, having to take care of this new bundle of joy, my older daughter, and my partner all at the same time was making me feel nauseated.

In the blink of an eye, I went from this happy, independent, single mom, to becoming pregnant with a new boyfriend of two weeks, moving an hour away, starting a new job, and giving birth to my second daughter. The darkest and scariest clouds rolled in over my life.

I'm not sure if these events are responsible for my mental health struggles, or if it was the nonstop arguments between the father of my older daughter. Maybe it was the Pitocin given to me prior to giving birth, maybe it was hormonal imbalances… Or was it my beautiful soul telling me I was not on the right path with my life?

I always said *everything happens for a reason,* or *we chose to live the path we are on.*

But why was I feeling this way? Why did I choose this path at this moment? *This is not fun at all, I don't feel like myself at all, where has Caro gone?*

In my mind this was not how it was supposed to go at all. I had it all planned. When I gave birth to my oldest daughter, Summer, it went well, and I got back to my normal self and life in no time.

In fact, it went so well that I had planned to give birth to this new baby, Lexa, naturally at home.

And I envisioned myself playing baseball that same summer.

I soon found out that sometimes we have no control over life events.

BACK HOME

I had no appetite, and just the smell of food made me feel sick. Within the first couple of days postpartum, I had already lost all of my baby weight. This was fantastic for the physical appearance, but inside it was killing me.

Baby Lexa was constantly latched to me, and I was surviving on protein drinks to make sure I had enough calorie intake for myself and the baby.

Hot summer days were here. The house had no air conditioning, and soon the lack of sleep caught up with me.

One night I started shaking, trembling from the inside. Plus I had the chills and my vision was getting blurry. I remember coming out of the bathroom holding on to the railing and screaming to my partner to dial 911. I thought I was dying.

I was lying naked in bed, pale and afraid. Paramedics arrived and took me for an ambulance ride to the ER with the baby on top of me. She couldn't stay behind, since she was breastfeeding and we had no formula for her at home. And to be honest, I didn't want to leave her behind. Just the thought of leaving my daughter, Summer, again and going to the hospital was haunting me. I always felt like she was put aside because of her new baby sister.

The next day I saw the doctor for less than five minutes and got discharged from the hospital right away. The doctor said my bloodwork was fine, that nothing was wrong with me.

I wanted to scream and knock him down.

Something was so wrong inside of me. *I feel awful, I am going crazy, please help me!*

- Have you ever been so mentally and physically tired, but can't fall asleep?
- Have you ever counted the hours before your baby goes back to bed?
- Have you ever counted millions of sheep jumping over that damn fence?
- Have you ever been so scared to be alone?
- Have you ever had a phobia of knives?
- Have you ever felt drowsy like you were out of your body?
- Have you ever had panic attacks driving on the highway?

- Have you ever started making up weird scenarios, stories inside your head?
- Have you obsessively thought about the worst outcome?
- Have you ever had thoughts about dropping your baby? Hurting your kids?
- Have you had muscle tension for no reason? Or tingling sensations or numbness? Or chest pain?

I had all these and *more*. One minute I was just fine and then bam, I had chills, felt nauseous, had diarrhea, had tingling all over my body, and my heart was racing. These are extra scary when it's nighttime and you are alone with two little kids.

While we slept, I had to have my laptop open to FaceTime with my partner while he was away for work. I was so scared to be alone. I soon started to stay with my in-laws when my partner Alain was away.

Even if you know you would never harm your child or yourself, it's very upsetting to have these thoughts and you feel ashamed to even be capable of these thoughts.

And how do you go about sharing these awful thoughts with your friends, your family? I tried sharing without going into detail with my midwife and close family members, but I always heard, "Oh yeah, it's the baby blues, talk to yourself, and it will go away."

Baby blues my ass! I knew it was way more than that because I was the one having all these thoughts and scenarios in my head. But if I shared them openly, I wondered, *Will I be placed somewhere? Will I lose my kids? Will I be left behind?*

The thought of my kids without their mother was killing me inside.

There are many reasons why moms don't want to share what we are going through and verbalize our strangest thoughts and images in our heads:

- We don't want to scare the other children
- We're terrified of having our children taken away from us
- We don't want to be considered dangerous
- We think we will get sent away
- We don't want anyone to think we are bad mothers
- We are embarrassed and can't handle it
- We don't want anyone to feel sorry for us
- We think it will go away on its own
- We don't want to be put on medication
- We don't know who to tell or share this with
- We feel very alone
- We feel embarrassed

With some online research, some guts to reach out and chat about how I felt online, I knew I had to go back to the hospital and get some help. I was so scared to go to see the same doctor that told me nothing was wrong with me. The day I decided it was time to go back and cry for help I was happy to see the face of a woman doctor in the ER. Amen!

Even if I didn't want to, I was at the end of my rope, and decided to put my pride aside and accept the help of medication. To help restore the serotonin in my brain, to help treat my panic attacks, improve my mood and appetite, and to decrease my weird fears, anxiety, and unwanted thoughts.

With the antidepressant treatment, some counseling coaching, turning to books, spirituality, and healing stones, I was able to cope more day by day, and live what I thought was going to be a normal life now.

May 2012: Not even a year after giving birth to my youngest daughter Lexa, I had total hysterectomy surgery. This was a choice I had made before getting pregnant with her. I had survived cervical cancer in the past and my tummy constantly hurt. Now my hormones were about to have another party! I was put on Estrogel® to reduce menopause symptoms.

March 2014: Still going strong, fighting my little monsters from time to time with the help of Zoloft®, I was living what I thought was a good and normal life. But when I look back now, I realize I was still living in survival mode and not thriving at all.

And then lightning struck again! This time it was not me but my husband who was fighting for his life. He was diagnosed with a brain tumor—cancer.

Why?

I remember calling my mom and telling her I was too young to lose my husband. I didn't want to be a widow at thirty-one years old!

Another life lesson was about to be taught. I completely lost myself trying to be the strongest to help him fight for his life, while trying to still find the old Caro I had lost way back in 2011 that I never truly got back.

Brain cancer sucks and can change someone's personality in an instant. When the tumor burst it created an uncontrollable hemorrhage, and I lost the man I married. He survived but was a man I no longer recognized.

I tried getting back the man I married in December 2012 with lots of hidden sadness covered up with a big smile and laughter. Living with a person with a brain tumor can be very difficult to accept and can change your life in so many ways. It can have a significant impact on your social, physical, and emotional well-being.

I turned to the arts to alleviate my ongoing anxiety, and I was able to hide my pain and sadness in the most beautiful art creations. But then I also turned to food for comfort.

TIME TO SHINE!

In 2016, I had my last big panic attack while driving home from work. I had to park the truck and dial 911.

This is when I made the decision to quit my job and heal my mind, body, and soul. I had had enough! I was too young to feel like this and I was supposed to be enjoying life to the fullest and not just surviving and hurting like I was.

I started reading the book *The Secret* by Rhonda Byrne, followed by her other books, *The Magic* and *Hero*, got my hands on *You Can Heal Your Life* by Louise L. Hay, started studying *Angel Numbers* by Doreen Virtue, and totally opened up with my spirituality.

This is when I had an aha moment where I knew for sure there was more to life than merely accepting my life's circumstances.

I switched from pessimist to optimist.

I went from black to rainbow.

I started making affirmations day and night:
    I am choosing to be happy right now.
    I can get through this.
    I breathe in confidence and exhale fear.
    I am grateful to see another day.
    My challenges bring me opportunities.
    I am safe and grounded.
    I am creative and joyful.
    I speak my truth.
    I am intuitive.
    I am not my anxiety.
    My anxiety is a liar.
    I am enough.
    I am fearless.
    I was not made to give up.
    I am healthy.
    I am alive.
    Abundance is drawn to me.
    I inspire others.

I forgive myself.
I forgive others.

I started listening to YouTube guided meditation channels and soon found out that you really start healing your life when you make small positive changes to it every single day.

I learned more about who I really was. I am an artist, an empath, and I love helping others.

I also discovered that I liked to be home, and I wanted to earn an income working from home.

I learned I could create the life that I truly wanted, with personal freedom. Nobody could stop me.

In late September of 2016, as I was scrolling through my social media one morning, I saw a post on Facebook that soon became the turning point that led me to a beautiful and magical transformation.

"Change your health, change your wealth, change your life" was written on the post.

It was a blue box of hope that soon gave me new wings to fly!
I started this new healthier journey on October 4, 2016.
In eight days my foggy thoughts lifted up, I regained some incredible natural energy, all my discomfort in my body was gone, I was sleeping better, and I was finally seeing the magical light at the end of this super long dark tunnel I was in.
With all the emotional eating I had been doing in the past, this new healthier lifestyle helped me lose nine pounds of emotional junk in those first

eight days, nineteen pounds of stuck emotions in sixteen days, and a total of twenty-seven pounds in two and a half months.

I had prayed for a healthier body, I believed in me, and I made it happen. I also prayed to live an abundant life in the comfort of my home. And I made that happen as well. This blue box of hope had an amazing opportunity attached to it and it was open to everyone! So when I saw what this could do for me and my family, I went all in.

Since then I have been sharing some of my own past struggles and my blue box story with thousands of people all around the world, giving them hope and helping them change their lives like I have changed mine.

I now have over 320,000 reasons to smile. I have been to six all-expenses paid trips for two and I just earned my seventh trip, as I am writing this, to beautiful Los Cabos in January 2023.

I have fought many wars alone, most of them internally. I AM tough. I AM remarkable.

I AM NOW UNFUCKWITHABLE.

I AM A BADASS.

And so are you!

About Caroline

CAROLINE LEMIEUX was born in beautiful Northern Ontario, Canada.

An animal and nature lover, she is a proud mother of two beautiful daughters. She is also one of the craziest rock ladies out there!

In 2011 she was diagnosed with postpartum depression and generalized anxiety disorder.

While battling with her mental health and helping her husband fight cancer, she turned to mixed media arts for therapy, discovering a special gift she has. Caroline is now a mixed media artist. With some soul searching, she found a new passion for health and wellness and has since then become a success and health coach, an amazing cheerleader, and incredible team leader.

Every day she wakes up and cannot wait to help more people change their health and discover their true potential and endless possibilities.

CONNECT WITH CAROLINE

- Email: caro_merc@hotmail.com
- Instagram: carolinelemieux29
- Facebook: caroline.mercier.1232
- linktr.ee/Carolemieux

Erica B. Lopez

SURVIVING MY MOTHER'S DEATH

IMMINENT DEATH

In a dream I called her name
and she didn't answer
She was too far away
I could see her face floating

Lies upon lies

Why do people lie to children?
As if we are too young to know
"Your mom is going to be okay"
What does that mean?

THE Badass WITHIN

She has been hospitalized for months
Her white skin turning yellow
The grip of her hand weakening
She was cold, so cold

Barely breathing, she speaks,
"And my daughters, who is
Going to take care of my daughters
Who is going to…"

Silence and one last kiss
Reluctantly, her soul leaves
Leaving four children
Leaving her home; her life

What am I, a child, to do?
When death chopped my mother-bond
When death shoplifted
Love and stability
When death mugged
A mother who loved
Wrapped her in his cloak
And robbed her from me
and her other children

I was kicked into:
Neglect
Molestation
Abuse
Abandonment

SURVIVING MY MOTHER'S DEATH

Encased in the never-ending
Feeling of not being good enough
Believing all was my fault
Love shrouded and non-existent

How did I rise?
When at five, this was my lot
How did I build self-worth?
How did I learn to love?

When rocks were thrown at me
Bullying, insecurity, loss
Growing up quick
Knowing life is tethered with pain

How do I pick up the pieces?
Or do I build armor?
Hiding behind walls
Pain running through veins

Love isn't real
When the one love I knew
With unconditional acceptance
Died… and death won

ONE OF THE BIGGEST STRUGGLES IN MY LIFE has been surviving the death of my mother. Her death felt like a lightning bolt that made my life crumble to the ground. She died when I was five years old, and her death marked the trauma that was going to follow me for the rest of my life. Many people say that the sadness of death heals through time. But time reminded me that I would experience so many monumental moments without her, and that followed me through my sense of lack. For years, by wasting time and energy focusing on the fact that I did not have my mother, I lived an empty existence.

The beginning of my depression happened the moment she died. My father was an alcoholic, and her death was a major blow to his ability to function in life. The only hope he had to live was the four of us kids. My sister was three, I was five, my middle brother was seven, and my older brother was ten. My mother did everything when she was alive—took care of the bills, the children, and the housework. When she died, we lost the pillar of our family. My father did not know how to do anything but work, so it was a learning process to figure out how to function without our mother. My little sister was too young to go to school, and so my grandmother, at seventy-six, had to take care of an energetic little girl all day. It was very difficult for everyone.

While my mother was in the hospital being treated for cancer, there was a lot of help. But after she died, we didn't have a lot of people who could help us, and we were left in a vulnerable state. My father was mourning, and at the same time he had to figure out how to provide for his four young kids. My aunt and uncle took all four of us for the summer, and we had a great time while my father was trying to make sense of his life. We had to return to my father when school was starting, and he left my ten-year-old brother in charge. Our elementary school was within walking distance from our home, so every day my dad went to work, and my oldest brother was in charge of making sure we got to school. For a short period of time, we took care of ourselves with no adult supervision until my father came back from work after five o'clock.

The school staff was concerned about our welfare, and social services was called to take us away from my father. My father had to hire a live-in caretaker so that he could comply with the social services requirements. I know there are rules and there are requirements for taking care of children, but my father had to work, so he had to leave us with babysitters. Doing so left me vulnerable to teenage pedophiles. Different individuals sexually molested me on multiple occasions. I had no voice and did not know at five years old how to advocate for myself. Being sexually abused and not having a mother to help heal was very challenging. It took years for me to look at this part of my life, including going to group therapy and traditional therapy to heal from the residual trauma.

Growing up we were poor. My father did not know how to read and write, and so he had hard labor jobs. He was also a cement truck driver. Money was always tight because he didn't know how to manage his finances. He also had to pay for babysitting. We had so many struggles growing up, including often running out of gas or our vehicle would break in the hot El Paso sun. Social services finally backed away from us when my father remarried and our stepmother came to live with us. She was with us for about three years, but due to relationship problems, she and my father split up. My abandonment issues skyrocketed. I had a mother, and she left. No matter how many times you explain to a child that it is not her fault, somehow, I owned the breakup and carried that burden too. For some reason I felt that our stepmother left us because of me. I was somewhat rebellious and did not listen, so when she left, my already low self-esteem plummeted even further.

I entered middle school in deep poverty. All our appliances broke after my stepmother left. Our boiler broke, our refrigerator broke, and our washer and dryer broke. We lived in Texas, and we could not shower because the water was freezing cold. I think that is why I was voted ugliest girl. It was a cruel joke, and it was done right under our teacher's nose. At the end of the year, the teacher allowed us to make up "awards," and the kids planned it. One of the students took the teacher outside to talk to him, and the students on the podium called my name for the award for "Ugliest Girl." I got up and went to the podium. When the boys yelled, "Speech!" I said, "Thank you all for noticing."

I knew to never let them see me cry. I had to build an armor around my heart, and as much as it hurt me, I played along.

All these moments in my life dictated who I was going to become. I felt ugly and unlovable, and it took me years to overcome the damage that was done through this bullying. It was a gash in my heart that emptied out the love, and I could not carry or hold love because I felt so undeserving. *Where was I going to find love?* I had no one to talk to, so I carried all this pain alone. I tried to keep moving forward, but the depression was overwhelming. In the eighth grade, I dated a boy that I was sure would love me, but he left me for my friend. When that happened, I felt so much emotional pain that I began cutting myself with a razor blade. People often wonder why people do this. All I can say is I wanted the emotional pain to go away, and I thought the physical pain would numb the emotional pain. It is not an answer, and in the end, you are in double the pain.

I truly believe in therapy, and I feel that if a child grows up in an alcoholic home, they should be sent to Alateen (a teenage program of recovery for the families and friends of alcoholics) along with therapy. *How different would my life have turned out if I had just gone to therapy sooner?* I have no regrets, but whenever I have an opportunity to help a teen or child go to therapy, I advocate as much as I can because having someone to talk to (in addition to your parents) is easier than trying to navigate the hard stuff alone.

Living without a mother forced me to live life without that kind of emotional support. In my family, we were not taught to be vulnerable and share our emotions. We spoke about logistical things, but we never shared the sadness or loneliness we carried. It is absolutely possible to be surrounded by many people and feel so desperately alone. That is what happened to me.

All my friends had mothers, and I did not. It was so lonely. For prom or any formal dances I attended, it was my sister and I trying to get a dress together and do my make up. I did not have my mother to get me ready or to take pictures of me. I could not really talk to my dad, and my siblings were living their own lives; we were all in survival mode. The abuse, the dysfunction, and the alcoholism would dictate how I would relate to the people I dated. I had no self-love, no self-esteem. I believed I was created to be abused, so I repeated this cycle, not realizing that I was carrying a bleeding wound that began the moment I was emotionally, psychologically, and physically violated. My cycle was chasing unavailable men and tolerating unacceptable behavior. My belief was that if a man needed me, he would not leave me. I was constantly dating men who would inevitably betray me, never realizing that these betrayals were linked to being molested as a child.

I learned all these connections in a support group called SAnon, a support group for friends and family members or people who have been affected by a sexaholic. I believe that the boys who molested me were also likely molested, exposed to porn, or were in some way negatively affected in their childhood regarding sex, and that is why they victimized me. This abuse caused me to repeat the same patterns with the men I would find myself in relationships with. In my relationships, it was always one of two things: either cheating or alcohol abuse. I was molested and that was a sexual betrayal, and when men cheated on me, that was another sexual betrayal. I repeated this pattern, not realizing it was rooted in me during my childhood. My father was an alcoholic, and I repeated that pattern too, dating excessive drinkers.

These patterns followed me throughout my life because I married a man who was both an alcoholic and a serial cheater. It was extremely difficult to heal and let go of the marriage because I was holding on to the patterns of my childhood. The fact that my mother died fueled my abandonment issues, and because I did not heal from my childhood molestation, I kept holding on to a dead-end marriage.

I always wished for a mother who could give me guidance, and I always felt inadequate because I didn't have that. I had to learn everything myself. I did get some help from my mother-in-law, but I always felt judged and unworthy. For years, I felt the pang of loss for my mother. My life was empty and unfulfilled because of my limited mentality of seeing the glass half empty. I did not want to see how my life had some elements of fullness, regardless of the dysfunction. There were parts of my life that were joyous, and I often took those parts for granted because of my depression and jaded thinking.

It was not until I was graduating with my master's degree that I realized I had succeeded even without a mother. I remember when it hit me. Despite all the craziness in my life, I graduated with a master's degree, and nobody could take that away from me. I may not have had my mother, but throughout all those moments she was always with me. Her death may have left me feeling empty, but it taught me love, compassion, and resilience. Even though I missed out on having her physically here in my life, I could call to her and know she was there in another realm.

We are all going to suffer loss and death, but we have to rise above the hurt and trauma and make our loved ones proud. Love never dies, and our loved ones exist in that love and watch us as we go on in our lives. When we have moments of hurt, they are there. When we have moments of celebration, they are there. We cannot focus on how we lost them. We must focus on how we *had* them. I may have had my mother for a very short time in my life, but I know she loved me. Her death resulted in me being strong and resilient. I could no longer waste my energy focused on what I lost. I needed to focus on all she left me in her short time with me.

Through loss and death, we are left with priceless memories and priceless lessons. Our loved ones never leave us, and we must embrace the life we had with them rather than focus on what we lost in them. Even though I did not grow up with my mother physically, she was with me every step of the way, and I know she looks down on me from heaven and is proud of me. I had a mother who loved me, and the love that she left in me was enough for me to rise through the pain and trauma and overcome. Shifting our focus and reframing our beliefs is so impactful because it is our perceptions that truly create our reality.

Recognize that we all need support and help at times, and if you seek help, you will find it. There are so many resources for healing. It is up to you to take the first steps. You can search for healing energy videos, meditations, yoga, and 12-step groups that can open your world to healing. You need to ask the universe for answers, and when it responds, you must take action.

For things to change, you need to take three steps.

1. The first step is building awareness of the help you need.
2. The second step is accepting where you are.
3. The third step is taking action toward healing.

I really want to emphasize being gentle with yourself. Healing is a process, and it takes time. Always remember that you are exactly where you are supposed to be, and as you continue on your way to healing, inspire others with your actions.

I strongly believe that every time a person heals, they are opening a road for others to follow suit. When you let go of your abuser, you are a pioneer opening the road to healing for the people who came before you and those who will follow you.

Every time you stand up, advocate for yourself, and speak your truth, you are creating a butterfly effect for others to do the same. We no longer have to suffer in silence. We can rise and overcome. No matter what happens to you, there is always something to be grateful for. When you focus on what you do not have, you fail to see the gifts of what you *do* have.

I want you to know that if you have lost loved ones in your life—they are with you. They are up there cheering and rooting for you to find peace, love, and healing. Our loved ones would not have wanted us to carry the gaping hole of their death. They would have wanted us to rise, be strong, and follow our goals and dreams.

About Erica

ERICA LOPEZ is an English high school teacher who has taught for twenty-four years. She is dedicated to helping and empowering her students, teaching them English by using life lessons as examples. Erica is a speaker, author, and life coach, and her goal is to help others find love within themselves and to find peace. She feels teens and kids need to be understood, and she dedicates her work to teach students that they need to reframe the struggles they have in their lives. As a psychic/medium, Erica helps people connect with their loved ones and find peace in their passing. She is an energy healer and a chakra specialist who helps people connect to their higher selves. Also a poet, Erica feels that poetry can help people heal their inner-selves. She is currently in the process of publishing her poetry book, *My Silent Voice Unleashed*.

CONNECT WITH ERICA

- Website: ericalifecoaching.com
- Email: ericablopez39@gmail.com
- Instagram: erica_lopez74
- Facebook: ericalifecoaching
- TikTok: ericalopezthree7s

Melissa Mae

SUCKER PUNCHED

> *"Getting knocked down is a given. Getting up and moving forward is a choice."*
> —Zig Ziglar

SUCKER PUNCHES, true to the name, come out of nowhere. They suck—big time! With a punch to the gut or to the face, the intent is to take you out. No forgiveness. Just a brutal shot determined to lay you flat on your back and put you to sleep.

As a fighter, you will without question get hit. At times, those hits come in the form of a *sucker punch*. When you put yourself in the ring or on the battlefield, when you decide to go to war, taking damage is just the name of the game. This is a guarantee.

As an entrepreneur, athlete, high performer, or an individual living life to its fullest, you are asking to get hit. It is just the way the game is played. However, how you choose to respond to these battle wounds will determine your destiny.

Sucker punches and hits come in all shapes and sizes. You are likely experiencing one right now. Whether it is a breakup, a divorce, or a disagreement in your relationship with your partner. Maybe you are treading through the perils of being a parent. Your professional environment could have you questioning life choices and dreading getting up in the morning. Were you just fired? Or need to fire someone in your life? Did life unexpectedly take someone special from your world without giving you notice first? Were you or a family member just diagnosed with a disease that has you on your knees, asking why? Has a project or business that you have poured your entire world into just gone up in flames or flooded you in debt? Has a vision you had for your life as an athlete been ripped from your soul due to injury or accident?

This list could continue for pages.

Sucker punches are real. Taking damage while in the ring is going to happen. I am no stranger to this danger and have taken my fair share of hits, just like you have. This is our real life. As fighters, we asked to be placed in the ring. As warriors we signed up for battle. We decided to fight. We have been chosen to go to war. We willingly signed our name on the dotted line, asking the universe to test us.

You may be an amateur fighter entering the ring for the first time. I applaud your courage. This decision to fulfill your destiny takes gumption and faith. You have chosen to be one of the few that refuses to live a life of mediocrity. You have the emerging mind of a fighter.

You could be a seasoned fighter. As a seasoned fighter myself, I stand to my feet and applaud you. You have already embraced the suck and continue to make the decision to fight, knowing this is not the easy path but one much of the population has avoided. However, you have set your focus on becoming a champion. The best damn fighter out there, with a purpose of reaching your potential every day, and claiming that champion title.

Take a moment and visualize with me now the last time you were sucker punched. The pain may be as real as right now. The confusion could be surrounding you as you dig deep into the depths of these words. Your heart could be aching, your ego bruised, your eyes swelling from tears. The pain is real. The disappointment looks back at you in the mirror. Your heart speeds up and your body becomes uneasy recalling the details. Sick to your stomach, you find it difficult to get out of bed. Hunched over, you fall to your knees and utter, "Why me? What did I do to deserve this?" The questions continue to race through your head. Full of doubt and insecurity, you question your faith, your strength, your ability to get up, your purpose (if you even know what that is). Getting hit *hurts*.

Getting sucker punched can take the life out of you. Like a squall on a sunny day, storm clouds cover your world. The winds are strong, the snow begins to disrupt your sight, and you are left in a state of alert. The radios urge you to take cover. Your phone beeps with a notification of what's to come. The desire to escape back to your comfort zone immediately enters your mind as the best choice, the easy option. And honestly, that's what most people will choose. This is a storm of catastrophic proportions; your world feels like it is ending. It is the perfect storm and others would completely understand your choice to return to comfort and status quo, to follow the sheep and settle in a land of mediocrity, a safe place, a shelter.

Your hope is diminishing, your heart is aching, and you are mentally, physically, and emotionally drained. It may seem like you have been fighting in this battlefield of desolation for what feels like forever. You beg for the round to be called. You want the pain and discomfort to end.

You are at a point where you must decide. You can stay where you are and lose the round by submission. Let that bell ring and watch as the referee raises the hand of your opponent, who won by hard work, sacrifice, resiliency, and faith.

Despite the damage, warnings, and chaos happening around you, you can choose to listen to the small voice inside your head that reminds you that you are a fighter. That your destiny is on the other side of this storm. And, most importantly, that you are not alone.

Compounded over time, these sucker punches, hits, self-inflicted challenges, or life's unexpected knockouts have a way of taking a toll. You are human. Part of becoming a champion, making it to the top, requires that you continue to train yourself and equip yourself with the necessary tools to navigate these attacks.

Conversely, not knowing how to navigate through these challenges after getting sucker punched will leave you hunched over on the ground, falling back into unhealthy patterns and bad habits, or throwing in the towel and giving up. The ripple effect this has on your life keeps you from reaching your true potential, your champion status, and fulfilling your destiny.

Like any champion that has weathered the storm, so can you.

No one is excluded from the list of having the opportunity to come across challenges, storms, and sucker punches. In fact, those of us with a bigger calling will find that we have more ring time. Those of you who have accepted the journey to become a champion will find yourself living on a battlefield. This should not scare you but excite you. You are destined for greatness. You have been appointed and are protected by a greater source to have a massive impact during your short time on this planet.

I am no stranger to challenges, knockouts, and storms. Honestly, I feel as if God has placed his hand on top of my fragile head and said, "My dear, you will face a multitude of challenges." Mind you, as you will notice later in this chapter, he also said, "My dear, you will overcome and conquer this challenge, you are a fighter. And I have got your back." Pretty powerful person to have in your corner, right?

The last words she uttered to me were "I love you." Over the phone, in another state, from a hospital bed, my mom was out of my reach. "My head hurts so bad, I love you," she uttered. I knew something wasn't right as I begged her to get the nurse's attention. "Mom, I love you, please let me talk to the nurse."

Growing up in a single-parent household, my mom and I were a team. We looked after each other and my three siblings. After graduating high school,

I joined the military. Leaving home, the burning desire to take care of and provide for my mother and family did not change. This was the driving force, the "what" that woke me up in the morning as my mission.

I felt helpless in this situation. Begging for the nurse's attention, relentlessly calling the hospital, only to finally be greeted by a nurse on the other line with my worst nightmare.

My mom. My rock. Was no longer here.

Out of nowhere, right to the liver, this was the punch that left me barely breathing. I curled over just in time to take a round kick to the face. Knocked out. Put to sleep. I lay in a pool of my own blood on the battlefield, curled up like a fetus. This was a pain like I have never experienced before. An opponent far advanced beyond my years, an enemy no one should have to cross paths with.

It was not until hours later that I received the details about my mom's headache. She had checked into the hospital for a routine back surgery. After completion of the surgery, my mother had been given medication to help with the pain. Unfortunately, the medication the hospital administered interacted adversely with another medication she was on, which led to the headache and ultimately, her going brain dead.

In disbelief, I packed up my family and headed to Utah to survey the scene for myself.

Entering the hospital felt like I was dreaming. I was still figuratively in the fetal position, hoping to wake up and find out this was all a bad dream. There was no way this could be real life. My mom was just forty-eight.

Confusion and heartache ran deep through my mind and body as I walked into the hospital room. In disbelief, I stared at my mom on the hospital bed, alive only by machine. I fell to my knees with my arms grasping toward her, begging God to please let her wake up. Tears poured from my eyes. *This is not fair! We are not done yet!*

My immediate and extended family were nowhere to be found. Their retreat from the battlefield, leaving me alone, would come to haunt me for years. I had no allies. There was no one in my corner. Left alone on the battlefield, I stood there in front of my mother's lifeless body with one last question to answer.

Making the decision to turn off the machines was one of the hardest questions I have ever had to answer. Standing there waiting for her to breathe on her own, the seconds seemed like hours. My world stopped. The crowd went silent. The sound from the knockout could be heard across the arena.

The round, the fight was over. I had fallen.

My biggest driver in life, my why, was to be able to provide for my mother. To finally give her a break from all the hard work and sacrifices she made for us. I wanted to take away her pain. I wanted to give her a better life. My fighting back against generational poverty, abuse, and violence was abruptly halted.

The bell rang before I could put in enough work to take her out of the fight. I not only lost the round, but I felt like I had lost the battle. I wanted so badly to never wake up. Life seemed so unfair. This was a hit I did not think I could rise from.

Have you ever felt that way? Like you wanted to give up? Like you could not get up? Maybe you felt like the message was clear; it was time for you to throw in the towel. Ring the bell. Quit. Give up. Have you been sucker punched so hard by this thing we call life that all you want to do is curl up and disappear?

This was one of those moments for me. This is one of the fights that many of us will find ourselves in. Where the odds are stacked against us. These battles are not uncommon and must be fought from the front lines.

> *"Our greatest glory is not in never falling, but in rising every time we fall."* —Confucius

My son had been born just six weeks prior, and my daughter was just four. My husband had just deployed. My younger brother, just fourteen, would now grow up with no mother or father. I was determined to not let them be casualties of this battle.

I had to get up. I had to wrap up. The fight must go on, and I was determined to lead from the front. There were no other options. No plan B. The mission, my why, must be completed.

I packed up our belongings in Las Vegas and my little family moved to Utah. The six months I spent in Utah handling my mother's affairs would be one of the most challenging times I have ever experienced. I did my best to keep it together and raise my young family during the day, surrounded by memories of her everywhere I turned. Nightly, I would cry myself to sleep in immense pain and heartache. I was walking through the battlefield, bleeding shame and bruised in regret. The days seemed long and unforgivable. "If only" consistently filled my thoughts. I was too late, and now I felt like I was paying the price.

It would not be until six months later that we would return to a somewhat normal routine.

My world shifted dramatically. Going through such a traumatic experience at such a young age, alone, forced me to step into the ring and fight. It required me to find solutions to unimaginable challenges. I had to dig deep and find strength. Had I not done so, I would have been left dead on that battlefield next to my mom. I refused to allow there to be two casualties. I know my mom would want me to rise up and fight. And so, with what was left in me, I fought.

Regularly, in the back of my head, I heard my mom's voice. A lot of my ability to navigate this situation I attribute to her and the example she set for me as I grew up. My mom was a servant leader. She always put others before herself. This situation could not be about me. My focus was on the mission. A skill I learned from my military career was to focus on the mission. Coupled with servant leadership, that became my solution. Impact and damage to my brother and children needed to be minimized. I had been hand selected for this mission, and it was a position only I could fulfill. Welcome to destiny.

When you put others first, despite your own feelings, the situations you are facing become easier to swallow. I am not saying it was easy. As Les Brown would say, "If you can look up, you can get up." Please, *choose* to get up and fight.

Chances are likely you are in the middle of what can seem like the fight of your life. Your fight is live and being shared on ESPN now. Amid what could be your last round, you picked up this book in hopes of finding a prescription for your pain. Your energy is depleted. Blood, sweat, and tears have significant meaning to you. You do not look like yourself or feel like yourself. Praying for reinforcements, this is not how you thought your life would play out.

Sucker punches, true to their name, come out of nowhere. An unexpected hit to the gut, or the liver, or straight to the jaw. Life will get its fair share of hits in. Some, like the jab, are meant to distract you or get your attention. Others can come as a powerful cross to the face, intended to knock you out if you're not prepared.

Regardless of the size of the punch, getting hit does damage. It will make an impact on you and those around you based on your response. These hits and battles will make or break you.

My purpose is to not only help you take hits with grace and gratitude, but to equip you with the techniques to get back up on your feet and fight back. You may be knocked out by a TKO (total knockouts). This is the lifeline to get you back up and back in the ring fighting.

You may be gasping for air right now or feeling a bit delirious. Maybe you don't even feel like you can get up, and reading this book is your last call for help. I get it. I feel you. I know it hurts. But pain is temporary.

I promise you, there is a fighter within you. We just need to peel back the layers, rebuild, and ignite your inner champion. Suffering exposes us to our highest selves. Getting knocked down is a given. Getting up and moving forward is a choice. I encourage you, I plead with you now, to make the choice. Choose you. Choose the destiny you are meant to fulfill. Fight.

About Melissa

MELISSA MAE found herself on the battlefield early in life. Raised by a single mother, growing up in poverty, Melissa learned the power behind hard work. She joined the United States Air Force right out of high school to put an end to the generational curse. Separating from the military as a combat veteran, she continued into the civilian realm where the battles followed. She could go into detail about failed marriages, abusive relationships, loss and so much more, but what matters is how she turned into the fighter within.

She lives every day true to her authentic self as a fighter, servant leader, serial entrepreneur, high-performance coach, speaker, author, athlete, and mother. She is grateful for the opportunity to teach others how to walk into the ring of life with their head held high and knock out every obstacle that stands in their way.

CONNECT WITH MELISSA

- Facebook: Melissa Mae Lantz
- Instagram: melissa_mae_lantz
- Website: melissalantz.com
- Email: melissa@melissalantz.com

Nicole Nohl

EMBRACE THE BAREFOOT MOMENTS

IN 2005, I embarked on a journey to improve my public speaking skills because I had let fear get the best of me during a job interview. I enrolled in the Dale Carnegie course, *How to Win Friends and Influence People*. In that course, I was introduced to the following story, based on *The Star Thrower* by Loren Eiseley.

> One day a man was walking along the beach when he noticed a boy picking up and gently throwing things into the ocean. Approaching the boy he asked, "Young man, what are you doing?" The boy replied, "Throwing starfish back into the ocean. The surf is up, and the tide is going out. If I don't throw them back, they'll die."

> *The man laughed to himself and said, "Do you realize there are miles and miles of beach and hundreds of starfish? You can't make any difference."*
>
> *After listening politely, the boy bent down, picked up another starfish, and threw it into the surf. Smiling at the man, he said; "I made a difference to that one."*

During the start of the pandemic in 2020, this story gained more importance.

Through the journey of life we can periodically be any one of these characters: the starfish, the dreamer/boy, or the witness/man. At times we might be the starfish, stuck in a situation of life that seems unbearable. We are out of our natural environment, and it is complicated to get back into the water or the groove and flow of life. Other times, we could be the dreamer who wants to make a difference, show up, and be of service to help someone back into abundance. Or we are a witness who makes a choice when seeing dreamers to encourage and support or to be a distraction, spread negativity, and hinder the success of others. Today, which are you and who do you have around you?

BEING THE STARFISH

Sometimes, we all need a hand.

My grandma Irene, a tremendous influence in my life, passed away in July 2020 after a surgery. This woman, who spent ninety-two years of life being active in church, dancing, cooking, agriculture, woodworking, crafting, and yard work, was also my childhood neighbor who helped me navigate life. Writing about this loss shakes me up and my eyes leak with loving memories.

Because she passed at the beginning of this awkward pandemic, we were limited in what we could do to celebrate her life. It was difficult to gather to tell stories and share memories. We had to wear masks and stay six feet apart, and no testing or vaccines were available yet. When our family began the daunting task of sorting through her years of belongings, treasures, and memories, we had to adjust our methods to complete those things. Our family was torn for a second time because some people followed the mask and distance recommendations tightly while others had a different practice. The struggle was, we were all grieving. The heart of the matter was that we needed to hold each other while falling apart but we couldn't find common ground to do so. By December, I knew the sadness of her passing was consuming me, so I decided to go to a counselor. We met weekly to help me find a new pattern of thinking and discover what life was again. I was referred to additional experts in areas that have helped me become a better person. I am an amazing creature like a starfish. Every once in a while, I need a helping hand. With a helping hand I learned that times of being stuck in the sand are only temporary. *You* can do this too!

BEING THE DREAMER

Some people cross our lives for a day, a season, a reason, or a lifetime.

There are blessings I can't measure. Several co-authors of this book have enabled me to be like the dreamer. Marie-anne Rouse, who has been in my network for a few years is responsible for recruiting and connecting me with this collaboration.

Liz Benecke-Wipfli rallied a group of people from vastly different backgrounds during the pandemic to do something about the mask shortage. The number of volunteers was extraordinary, including people who donated fabric, sewed the masks, and delivered them all over our region. I humbly lent my computer skills to the team to keep communication flowing, record the daily processes, manage social media, and organize the database.

Erin Baer has supplied her book to women's shelters. Her book is helping women overcome the darkest of circumstances. It has been my pleasure to be a sponsor so that copies could be provided to shelters in my state.

Making a difference happens in moments that we must seek out, embrace, and keep going. Collect lots of them!

BEING THE WITNESS

In the story, this character can be a motivator by speaking about limitations. There will be people who come along and try to take you off track. What will you do? Will it be a distraction or refocus on the goal? Are there people you can influence? In what ways must we observe ourselves? When life gives us the moments of meaning and purpose, what will we do with it?

The place I worked through college also was the company where my dad worked. On most days, he was my boss. I was the final inspector of each plastic-wrapped food product box before it was sent to the freezer and then the customer.

The manufacturer who printed the packaging had made an error—the imaging was twisted. Looking sloppy and slanted, I rejected the packages. The machine operator got so mad at me that she called the boss (my dad) into the room (it felt like being sent to the principal's office). We discussed it, and I was told I should let them through. I knew that as a customer, that misprint would make me skip over the boxes. On my lunch break, I took some of the sloppy boxes to the supply purchasing office to tell them it was unacceptable printing. They reviewed multiple cases, which had over 1,000 pieces per box, finding the problem in all of them. This resulted in my company getting a refund for faulty products from the printer. I was the dreamer looking out for my starfish (the customer), and the witness (my boss/dad) didn't like my actions. I put my head and heart into making a difference, doing what was right even when it was hard, rather than listening to the negativity around me.

Once while sitting in church, I could hear someone near me softly crying. In the gentlest way, I handed her a tissue and my open hand to support her in this sorrow. My husband, who was sitting with me, didn't even know that she and I had this exchange. At a moment when we all stood, she tugged on my shirt, and we left. Once outside the doors, I gave her a super tight hug. She fell into a deep sob and thanked me for being there to support her. At the time I didn't know the circumstance that brought her this pain, but I was going to be there until the wave was gone. A thank you note arrived a few days later in which she mentioned she and her spouse were beginning the process of divorce and that day was especially rough. She said my silent embrace was a grace that gave her strength.

There will be times when the people before us need words or actions that show, "I believe in you. You have got this. Keep going."

How about you, reader? I believe in you! You are doing great with what you've got. Keep going!

My favorite wisdom from my grandfather Elroy and his spouse, Irene was that they love the poem about the man who dreamed he saw two pairs of footprints in the sand. One left by him, the other left by Jesus, walking by his side throughout his life. When he saw only one set of footprints, he asked Jesus about it. Then Jesus replied, "During your times of trial and suffering, when you see only one set of footprints, it was then that I carried you."

When life brings you trouble, get barefoot and go walking in the sand!

Embrace the moments when being you (a starfish, a dreamer, or a witness) makes all the difference.

About Nicole

NICOLE J. NOHL is a mother goose to anyone who crosses her path for an hour, a season, or a lifetime. She is proud of being a rockstar wife, bonus mom, extraordinary friend, family historian, and greeting card queen.

She grew up on her family's dairy farm in Wisconsin. That lifestyle influenced her to pursue a bachelor's degree in agricultural education. She taught agriculture for elementary and high schools for eight years. In 2005, she took the transformational Dale Carnegie Course to gain public speaking skills and live the principles of *How to Win Friends and Influence People*. She is blessed to work part time for #TeamAloha as a digital live online producer and customer experience coordinator.

She began a connection advisor career in 2007, with the relationship marketing company SendOutCards, now with even more product lines as an affiliate of Greener Still. Nicole is dedicated to coaching people on making intentional connections through personalized greeting cards.

She has resided near Green Bay (da Packers) since 2008 when she married Kevin C. Ress.

Her volunteer activities include being a wedding host for their church, presenting weekend retreats for Marriage Encounter, serving on a computer task force for Wisconsin Face Mask Warriors, and is active with Alpha Omicron Pi alumnae sisterhood.

In her free time, she enjoys making memories with her family, her adult stepkids, friends, and rescue dog, Lexi.

CONNECT WITH NICOLE

- LinkedIn: nicolenohl
- SendOutCards: SendOutCards.com/u/26886

In Memory of Irene Kissinger

Susan Paxson

LIZARD BRAIN AND WIZARD BRAIN

AS A CHILD, I couldn't quite put my finger on it. On the outside, we looked the part of a well-functioning family—two parents and two daughters. I had the basics: food to eat, a bed to sleep in, and clothes to wear. We went on vacations. I didn't question that anything was ever wrong. But inside the house, a terrible, unpredictable monster lived with us: my father's *anger*. If I could avoid this monster's gaze, I was okay and could exhale quietly. I could survive this. *But how do you play the game with a monster who is always changing the rules?*

In third grade, it was finally my turn to be Student of the Week. My mom helped collect photos of our family. My dad loudly reminded me how priceless and irreplaceable those photos were. On the bulletin board, I looked like a normal child in a normal family. I got to fill out the interview page with my favorite foods, books, and movies. I felt seen and special for the entire week.

When Friday arrived, my material went into a file folder for me to take home. I gripped it in my arms as I took the bus to the recreation center for after-school care. It was a blustery spring day, and as I walked across the grass, a gust of wind blew a photo out of the folder. I panicked and dropped the whole folder of photos. The stack went whooshing up into the air in all different directions. My heart dropped into my stomach. I cried out, *"Oh, no! Someone help me!"* I tried to chase after them, hoping to reclaim one. *Just one.* Then I watched helplessly as my efforts to avoid my father's rage blew away with the wind.

It felt like I was frozen in time until my mom finally arrived. I had cried all afternoon: inconsolable, completely heartbroken and terrified about what would happen when my dad found out. I met her with red, puffy eyes and a tearstained face. She took me home. My dad *really* showed me how angry and upset he was. My fear was real: mistakes were not allowed, and this was a *huge mistake*. He screamed and screamed, and then he screamed at my mom for ignoring him and letting me take the photos to school. *Priceless! Irreplaceable!* His voice turned into unrecognizable, shrill screeches as he lost his mind over my carelessness. His fists shook, and he towered over me in physical terror and intimidation. On windy days, I sometimes *still* feel the painful pang of the *bad thing I did*. It haunts me.

As I got older, I expertly became invisible to avoid provoking his *anger* and its companion, *rage*. I did well in school and participated in several sports. Summer days were a blur of classes and after-school camps. But I couldn't shake the loneliness. Avoiding mistakes and flying under the radar became my full-time job. I took the public bus to the mall and the library, spending hours alone and disconnected. Somehow, I believed I was the only person who could take care of me, especially if I could control all of the details in my life. I would do it alone.

As I developed, I realized that my appearance was an asset, and I enjoyed the attention. I grew out my hair and landed my first boyfriend. It was the summer before my sophomore year. He was a senior at another school, who smoked and whose mom liked me. (I had set the bar pretty low.) I convinced my parents to let me go on a "camping trip" with his friends. Everyone at the house party knew what the *group plan* was for us: they gave us the bedroom. When it came time to go through with the plan, I changed my mind. I wasn't ready to give that part of myself to someone else yet. This wasn't the attention I had in mind.

Everyone at the house was a faceless stranger, and I didn't even know where I was. It felt like I was on another planet, and I just couldn't move or figure out how to get out of the bed. So, instead of making a scene and predicting how my parents would respond, I disconnected from my body as he raped me. That was my first time.

At the end of that school year when I stopped playing basketball in favor of joining the band again, my dad's response was, *"But you never practiced the trombone!"* At this point, I didn't give a fuck what he thought about my choices and decisions anymore. He wasn't someone I trusted.

Band saved me. I was always gone from the house, making music and taking part in something bigger than just me. I enjoyed the structure and thrived in the hierarchy. For the first time, I belonged and felt valued. And it provided me with a selection of high-quality boys from good families—I dated almost all of them. I became a regular guest at their houses: the Sunday pizza nights, the gourmet food, and the praying before the meals. I stayed until they asked me to go home.

Meanwhile, the clashes with my dad escalated and became violent. My escape would often be running out of the front door, almost all of the time without shoes. When I could drive, I would keep keys and my wallet close by in the case of the need for a hasty exit. Several times I spent a week or more at different friends' houses. During one particularly bad scene during my senior year, I dialed 911 and then overheard my father lie to the officer about the disturbance. *No one accidentally dials 911 and hangs up.* Disgusted by the hypocrisy, I moved out of the house for a month during my senior year. My mom finally convinced me to return home, but we never spoke about it again. I was holding my breath, waiting to escape. As I approached college and freedom, the only things I knew were that I was going to get out of Boulder in favor of Fort Collins, and that I would be in the marching band. I knew I had to get out of there. Home was not a safe place.

I loved living on my own and dated a lot. The marching band, once again, became my chosen family and my savior, so I majored in music. At twenty-four, I fell in love with and married a kind guy with a stable family. He was exactly the opposite of my dad. I graduated and got a teaching job in a small school district. But I struggled with stress and anger and unhappiness. After two years of marriage, my mother-in-law called my husband: *We think that she's not a good wife for you and that you should divorce her.*

After a year I got a different teaching gig, hoping to improve my wife skills. My mother-in-law patched it up with me eventually, but I still felt lonely and desperately wanted to belong. I thought that if I just tried harder, I would be able to manage stress and anger better. I wanted to be better so I would be loved.

When my husband graduated with a math degree, I resigned my teaching job and changed gears to become a photographer. I missed teaching and was lonely, so I took a one-year position at the same school he was teaching at. In August of that year, my mom was diagnosed with breast cancer. I shaved her head in October and met her at as many chemo treatments as I could. We never discussed her mortality, but my husband and I agreed it was probably a good time to start our family, in case she was on borrowed time. I got pregnant quickly. I was five months pregnant when my mom died: a year after her initial diagnosis. That time is mostly a blur of tears and numbness. I don't remember many details of her service or how my sister and I absorbed her possessions or slowly moved through the evidence of her life. I became a motherless daughter.

December 12, 2012: After many hours of unmedicated labor, I knew I was headed for a C-section. I told the nurse and my support team, and after a few more hours, they agreed with me. My son was born at 1:51 am on December 13th. The paradigm shift was that I was no longer in control.

Am I safe if I am not in control? It wasn't just about me anymore, and I began tightening my grip on control. I made my way through a stupor of grief and postpartum depression for months and months, just trying to keep both of us safe and alive. It never even occurred to me that I should have gotten any help. I began turning to stone.

Fast forward…

Today, I know that *my childhood influenced the choices I made.* I learned that fear and inconsistency compelled me to only trust what I could control and manage. My brain was often hijacked by the reptile lizard brain: the primitive fight, flight, or freeze response to navigate my father's abuse. I mastered the skill of reading emotions and became a highly sensitive empath. Hypervigilance and extreme caution calibrated my nervous system to operate normally with cortisol (the stress hormone) constantly in my bloodstream. I excelled with procrastination, urgency, and drama. The survival adaptations of perfectionism, intense punctuality, and workaholism actually merged themselves successfully into two careers that brought me a lot of joy. (And control!) On the outside, I was a highly functioning adult. But on the inside, I was a scared, confused, disconnected little girl.

I left my first husband for a man that I didn't mean to fall in love with. We were both looking for unattached fun, but I was fascinated with how he saw the world and the ideas he had. He opened up my world to possibility, and I began to feel joy. We dreamt about building a life together that would be different and amazing. As he loved me, I began to believe that I was worthy of love. And then he encouraged me to love myself. We bravely chose a different path because we could both see where it could lead. We blended our four kids (his three and my one) and our lives—in spite of the stigma and shame of this *bad thing we had done.*

This new life we made, though, still included my wounded, little girl brain in addition to the overwhelming stress and shame of our affair. I did what I knew, and during a fight one night, I ran out the front door without shoes or a coat. It was a November night, and he called the police because I was threatening to kill myself. My desperate cry for help was answered: I was handcuffed and driven in a police cruiser to the hospital for my own safety. Early the next morning I was admitted to a psychiatric hospital.

The seventy-two-hour hold turned into six days. It was our first wedding anniversary on the day I went home. We made plans for an eight-week inpatient treatment program in Kentucky, because I was more than the two of us could manage. I didn't have to hide from my childhood alone anymore. Learning about how my adaptations to survive had primed me for some numbing, addictive behaviors, I started a path in 12-step recovery. As I told my entire life story, I experienced unconditional love and support. I felt little glimmers of the serenity I was chasing, and it kept me hungry enough to continue.

I began building a tribe of people who would love me *exactly as I showed up*. Digging into the work was my only way out and through, so I stayed for twelve weeks. I was in Kentucky from the end of November through the middle of February—including my son's fifth birthday, my birthday, my husband's birthday, and all of the winter holidays. I worked on retraining my brain, understanding my traumas and triggers, and how to be flexible and loving toward myself. As hard and as painful as it was, it was the best thing that could have happened.

I continued to dig into my personal work when I came home. It's never really over and one doesn't really arrive, I discovered. So, I became curious and willing to explore more possibilities. Ketamine therapy[4] was very successful and opened my mind to more healing with unconventional chemicals.

My therapist asks me the hard questions. I now listen to my mind and body because the stress volume (cortisol) has been turned way down. And the answers are sometimes napping, dancing, or eating, depending on the question. I am doing the work, but I'm also thriving.

I owe so much of this expansion to my husband. He wasn't the lynchpin for my trauma healing—he was the catalyst: *A person or thing that precipitates an event.* He gave me space and time to look at the ugly parts of myself and improve them. His insights are often spot on, and I truly value being known to someone so intimately. We model a healthy partnership for our kids, and there is lightness and joy in our home. Our family motto is: *Always improving.*

In *wizard* brain, there is so much more space for moments of connection and retrospection than in *lizard* brain. There is quiet, peace, and creativity. I can look at my family and see how they need to be loved. It's actually really simple. *Meet them where they are.* In a connected state, I can weave a safety net for my kids instead of compelling them out of fear. Across a tightrope they walk, making their mistakes and learning from them with empathy instead of worry. They can build confidence because they have a wide net of safety beneath them. They will make decisions during calm instead of in panic. They are not protected from discomfort or stress, but they evaluate their choices in wizard brain instead of reacting from them in lizard brain. They live in resiliency.

If my children ever find themselves in messy, confusing situations, I hope they trust that they can reach out for help. I hope they believe me when I remind them that it's okay to call us and we'll come get them, no matter when and where. I hope they truly *know* that the brave choice to ask for help will

---

4   "Ketamine for major depression: New tool, new questions," Robert C. Meisner, MD, accessed July 22, 2022, https://www.health.harvard.edu/blog/ketamine-for-major-depression-new-tool-new-questions-2019052216673.

never be a higher price to pay than the consequence of staying silent. We're breaking the cycle of abuse and trauma with trust and connection.

Badassery is about knowing thyself. It is being willing to look into the dark corners and shadows and learn about those things. To learn about and acknowledge the abuse so that reactions can be rewired. To cast light into those dark corners with grace, kindness, and compassion for myself and my parents—after all, they did the best they could with what they had. To offer the little girl in me the same kindness, forgiveness, and unconditional love that I show my kids.

What I control now is how I show up. How I connect with people in my life. The work I've done with my demons and my traumas is worth the gravity, effort, and stamina required to dig even deeper. Because when I taste that peace; the flicker of hope, or the sun shining on my face, the ocean rushing between my toes, and the lightness, the beautiful shimmer of joy is what I crave. That is what I chase. That is what I live. That is what I share. Joy is badass.

About Susan

SUSAN PAXSON was born and raised in Boulder, Colorado, and graduated from Fairview High School. She earned her BA in Music Education from Colorado State University in 2005 (tuba). She enjoyed a successful career teaching band and orchestra for six years at several northern Colorado schools that included a 3A State Marching Band title at Windsor High School in 2011. While teaching music, she also started In Harmony Studios photography and was a fellow in CSU's National Writing Project Summer Institute in 2009.

In 2016, she moved to Superior, Colorado, remarried, and blended her family of four fantastic children, now thirteen, eleven, nine, and eight. She still works on personal growth and reparenting herself so that her kids will grow up *knowing they are loved for exactly who they are.*

Susan loves to use her skills as a photographer, seamstress, musician, and graphic designer to perform various feats of excellence and joy. She also seeks to make her home a place that feels like vacation, even on Tuesday nights between dinner, showers, and bedtimes. Her favorite way to relax is to play her ukulele.

Marie-anne Rouse

NOBODY KNEW

NOBODY KNEW.

Nobody knew that behind that closed bathroom door, the ninety-pound, frail body of a teenage girl was lying on the ground, silently sobbing.

Nobody knew that this teenager was feeling such despair and hopelessness that she couldn't see herself living through another day.

Nobody knew that as she sat up, she clutched in her trembling hands a full bottle of oxycodone.

Nobody knew this was the hardest experience of her life. She kept it secret for so long, just like she kept the rest of her past hidden from others, and herself. Yes, you have probably deduced that the girl I am talking about is me. That's not me today. I have learned from my experiences and the cost of keeping them a secret.

Before we go to where I am now, let us rewind the sands of time and go to where and when things began. Born in Brussels, Belgium, I always appeared to be a happy child while growing up. I was happy in many moments but had learned early on to keep everything bottled up inside because sharing my thoughts and feelings would only make life harder for me and those I loved. It was a self-defense mechanism that served me well… until that emotion-filled bottle was full and cracked. Maybe you can relate to keeping things under lock and key. You don't want to open that Pandora's box, not even for yourself, as you don't want to be reminded of the contents held within.

I have opened that box for myself, but the mind has a way of creating boxes within boxes. To this day, I see a box inside that has remained sealed, but the seal is leaking bits and pieces, with images and dreams resurfacing that make me wonder if that tiny box hiding deep in the back corner should even be opened. I don't have the answer to that yet.

I am not saying that I had a horrific life. I know there is always someone who has had a harder time.

Thankfully, I can say there were many happy times like learning how to ride a bicycle without the training wheels.

Happy times like sneaking out of school to go to the farm out back and feeding the bunny rabbits the clover flowers that the farmer had shown us they loved.

Happy times like flying to Spain as an unaccompanied minor and getting to help the flight attendant pass out the goodies being purchased on the flight. Oh my, how times have changed! Back then, they were called stewardesses and they would push a cart down the aisle with items available for purchase. There I was, my long, dark brown hair in two braids draped from one side to the other on top of my head like a headband, as proud as I could be while handing passengers their bagged purchases.

The happy times have been the stories I've shared with others over the years.

What I kept to myself, and over time buried in my mind's Pandora's box, were the not-so-happy times that came from being a child caught in the middle of a nasty custody battle and living in places where I witnessed, heard through the walls of my room, or experienced physical and mental abuse. I was that child who would get picked up from school in the middle of the day by someone else's mom, so I could stay at their home until the coast was clear for me to go home. I was that child who got picked up right outside of school and taken across the border against court orders. I was that child who was the youngest of her siblings, the one whose siblings kept her as safe as they could. I was that child hiding in the closet under the staircase, leaning against the water heater. I was that child who would shrink in fear at the sound of a certain type of car.

Did both of my parents love me? I am sure they both did. Yet, I felt like a pawn piece in a game of divorce chess and many things that took place should never have happened. Some people haven't learned not to hurt those you love or use them as pawn pieces to hurt someone else. Unfortunately, there are too many relationships that are that way. Without going into a whole discussion about relationships, there are relationships that even when love is present, it is not always in everyone's best interest to be present for one another. Being apart is best in some cases.

This game of divorce chess had some of our family move to a different country, which turned out to be not far enough. That is how some of us ended up moving to America… and no one could know. This meant we had to disappear without saying goodbye to anyone. As a preteen, there was a sense of excitement and adventure about it, but the hard part was having to leave without saying goodbye to our grandparents. The move to America was a fresh start. It was a new life, new language, new home, new schools, and eventually new friends. The emotional baggage and fears came along for the ride, along with the lies we had to tell because we didn't want others to know our story.

Six years later, I turned eighteen. I was officially an adult in America. I could vote. I could be independent. And that is when it hit me like a ton of bricks. Weakened at the knees, tears of relief streamed down my face as I tried to keep walking on my way to work. The experiences of the past eighteen years were finally over, and the next chapter of my life was beginning. *My life!* That feeling that I no longer could be claimed by someone else. I claimed myself. I was free.

Little did I know that those eighteen years were preparation for the hardest experience that would transform me into the person I was born to become. Little did I know that being able to set that baggage aside was to give me a chance to build up my physical and emotional strength. This was the calm before the storm. While I no longer had to keep secrets from the world, I didn't feel the need to share details of the past.

I started focusing on my dreams and enjoying what I was feeling was now *my* time. My time to live. My time to dream. My time to spread my wings and soar.

Later that year, the storm hit with unexpected force in the form of a phone call while I was at work. The voice on the other end informed me that my mother had been in an automobile accident. A hit-and-run accident caused her car to wrap around a pole. Emergency responders were able to get her out with the jaws of life. I was told that she was at the hospital and to get there as quickly as possible. They didn't know if she would make it. She made it through, and I became her caregiver. I would not have it any other way.

At the age of eighteen, I was a full-time caregiver, going to school, and going to work. I also became head of the household. Thankfully, the latter was without the financial responsibilities as my stepfather was working. He would also help in the evenings so I could get some sleep. Months of caring for others and keeping up with responsibilities and commitments took their toll. I was forgetting something extremely important. In order to care for others, I needed to care for myself. I didn't realize that caring for myself wasn't selfish, and would help me in caring for others.

I felt like I had control of nothing in my life anymore except for the food I ate. Or rather, the food I didn't eat. I lost roughly twenty-five pounds and became a ninety-pound shell of physical, emotional, and mental exhaustion. This brings us back to "nobody knew."

Nobody knew that thirty-plus years later, that once broken teenager now a thriving woman because in that moment that nobody knew—I saw a light in the storm.

It wasn't anything huge. But it was enough to help me find the inner strength to make it through another day.

And another.

And another, as the light in the storm grew stronger and stronger, and I released my inner badass!

I have realized that all the experiences I have had, even as a child, are experiences that I needed to have to become the woman I am today. I have realized that all the experiences were important for me to go through because I am meant to help others who are enduring their storm. Sharing my story has become the light through the clouds for many others, teens and adults, men and women.

Three things I know.

First, if you are going through a storm and your nest is being shaken, I want you to know that you are not alone and you are stronger than you realize. There is a badass within you waiting to be released. Second, I want you to remember that self-care is not selfish. Show yourself the love, care, understanding, and grace that you freely give to others. You deserve it. You are worth it. You matter more than you realize. And third, someone needs to hear your story. You may not know who yet, so I highly recommend that you get a journal and start writing down your story, events you remember, and emotions you feel and have felt. Not only can that help you in bringing clarity to your experiences and the possible reasons hidden within them, but it can also help you in processing and releasing the emotions attached to them. Then, when you share with someone who needs to hear your story, instead of feeling like a therapy session, you will be the light through their clouds because you too are a badass.

About Marie-anne

MARIE-ANNE ROUSE is a speaker, coach, best-selling author, and serial entrepreneur in the network marketing industry as well as the traditional business model. Originally from Europe, Marie-anne made her childhood dream a reality when she flew to Hawaii for her nineteenth birthday, moved there, and met the man who later became her husband. Besides loving to write, she loves to explore creative and artistic outlets such as playing with glitter, jewelry making, painting, and live theater, both behind the scenes and on stage. She is on a mission to inspire and motivate individuals whose nests have been shaken. She wants to help them let go in order to live and soar. Her purpose is to help others release their inner badass and find their own voice.

Her most recent works are *Resilience to Greatness, Mindset Reset*, and *Release Your Inner Badass.*

CONNECT WITH MARIE-ANNE

- Website: MarieanneRouse.com
- Facebook: marieanne.rouse
- TikTok: @client_retention_queen
- Links: mylinks.now.site

Karen Siliven-Monnier

ONE STEP AT A TIME

HOW DID I GET HERE? I thought as I took in the view from a wooden platform.

I am afraid of heights, yet there I stood, sixty feet in the air. I couldn't help but wonder about the transformation my life had taken in a span of three years.

Reflecting back, I didn't realize how isolated I had become until after my father passed away. During the last six months of his life, I was his full-time caregiver, chasing ambulances, rushing him to the hospital, and caring for him twenty-four hours a day when he was home. Until the early hours one morning, when Mom called and said she thought he had passed.

I sat on the side of his bed and held his hand. Waves of emotions flooded through my body, threatening to drown me, as tear after tear slid down my face. He had been through so much in those last six months, and I was with him through it all. We had laughed and yelled at each other. I had been his voice when he couldn't speak when the doctors had wanted to remove life support.

Dad's passing was one of those life-changing moments. My life had been wrapped around caring for him. Now that it was over, I was lost. I didn't realize then how badly childhood bullying had affected my life, leading me to a self-imposed isolation.

Being bullied throughout childhood and young adulthood had shaped my adult life. Not only did it come from kids; it came from teachers as well. During my fourth-grade year in school, the physical education coach seemed to go out of his way to make sure I felt like there was something wrong with me. One day, while my class was sitting on the bleachers before class, he walked by and stopped in front of me. He was holding a whistle attached to a cord and proceeded to twist it, then flick me with it. I wasn't acting up. I was sitting there quietly, and he hit me hard enough to make me cry. As tears streamed down my face, he ordered me to stop, walk outside the gym, and get a drink of water. I still do not know what provoked him or why he would even think that was acceptable behavior. It had a profound effect on me.

I wish I could say that was the only incident. Actually, it was just the beginning. Even after my family moved to a different school district, the bullying didn't stop. My first day in a new school, I was walking down the hall, when a boy from my class jumped on my back and would not get off. I had to walk backwards into a wall to get him off me. Each morning, I dreaded going to school because I knew what was waiting for me.

Once I graduated high school, I worked for my father on the farm. It was hard labor, but I loved it. After five years, I felt like I needed a change and went to a business school, which required me to move from home for the first time. I started school and entered the workforce. Attending classes full time and working forty hours per week built my confidence because I excelled at work and maintained a 4.0 grade point average. Suddenly, life was different. No longer subjected to bullying, I finally felt like I fit in.

Several years later and full of confidence, I went for a job interview. Throughout the process, all indications were that the job was mine. I could feel the excitement building, and then the final thirty minutes happened. The interviewer ended the session by taking the opportunity to belittle me in front of everyone. She heavily criticized the way I was dressed. I was professional, wearing a long skirt with a nice blouse. What was wrong with that? I am still dumbfounded by her behavior. All the confidence I had managed to build since high school was immediately destroyed. I was devastated. That night, I sat down and wrote a letter to that organization's directors telling them exactly what she did to me, the profound effect it had, and threatened to sue them for discrimination. I received a phone call from their attorney, profusely apologizing with a promise that I would receive a phone apology from the lady who conducted the interview. She never called.

Over the course of the next several years, I became a business consultant for organizations and set up a home office. For almost twenty years, that is how I conducted my career until I moved closer to my parents and became Dad's caregiver.

After Dad passed, I considered retiring. Returning to corporate work didn't appeal to me. Dad and I had planned to garden together. I could still do that in his memory, so I joined a master gardener's class. While I enjoyed it, I found myself wanting to be more involved, and could see myself doing presentations, training, and teaching.

It was a revelation. I was missing the type of work I had done for so many years. However, I couldn't see myself returning to the corporate environment.

Scrolling through social media one day, I noticed someone offering life coaching services, which was completely done online. *Oh, that's interesting,* I thought. *This is something I can do. Help people and coach from the comfort of my home office.*

But how does one become a life coach? I remembered a coaching certification course I had considered a few years before through the John Maxwell Company and decided to give it another consideration. I spoke with a program advisor to make sure I could do it from home and joined.

After a couple of weeks, during my onboarding session, I discovered that I would have to attend the actual certification event in Orlando, Florida *in person*. Fear gripped my soul. I couldn't breathe. *It was a live event?* And then it hit me. I had worked from a home office for twenty years, hardly venturing out in public. Paralyzed with fear, I had never thought about what this meant. But now it hit me like a ton of bricks. I was afraid of people. I had invested a small fortune for this certification, and in order to complete it, I would have to go to the certification event. *How will I get through this?*

I registered for the February 2018 event, and nervously flew to Orlando. The event was massive, with about 3,000 people in attendance. I soon discovered something about the John Maxwell Team. They are huggers. And I was horrified. Fear of people surfaced quickly and suffocated me. I didn't want to be touched, and everywhere I turned, someone wanted a hug. At the end of the first day, I returned to my hotel room in tears. *I've made a huge mistake,* I cried. *I can't do this. I can't handle this.* And I called home, with my desire to leave the conference and return to the safety and comfort of the four walls I had constructed around my life. Don't misunderstand me. Every member of the John Maxwell Team was loving and caring and oh, so friendly. But I couldn't handle it. The years of bullying had caught up with me and taken me down.

What am I going to do? I wondered as I sat alone in my hotel room. *What can I do? How can I get out of this and get home?* While sitting there contemplating my next step, I thought, *Well, what CAN I do?* Thoughts ran through my mind. *Go home. Stay and attend the conference. Run away. Stay.* It seemed too huge to decide. So, I asked myself again, *What CAN I do?* I could get ready for the conference in the morning, but I didn't have to attend. Fantastic. Then

I asked, *What's the next thing I CAN do?* With every task, every moment, I had to ask myself, *What's the next thing I CAN do?* And every moment, I did only the thing I had decided that I could do, until finally, I had to decide whether to go to the conference or not. *Now, what CAN I do? Well, I can get on the elevator and go to the hotel lobby.*

Success. *Now what CAN I do?* I could walk the long corridors to the location of the event. Again, success. That is how day two proceeded. Every moment, every step, I continually asked myself, *Now, what CAN I do?* Each time I would ask myself that question, I also gave myself permission to *not* be ok with any of this. I didn't have to stay. I didn't have to participate. It would be okay if I chose to stay holed up in my hotel room for the rest of the event. It would be okay if I chose to rent a car and drive home. It would be okay if I changed my flight arrangements and ran screaming back to the comfort of my home. Whatever I decided, I made up my mind it would be the right thing to do, and it would be okay. That was powerful. I had given myself permission to be okay with whatever I would decide. I felt in control of the situation instead of feeling forced to complete something. It was in my control and no matter what I decided, it would all be okay.

The internal struggle lessened, and I managed to get through the day. I felt liberated and realized I just might be able to get through the event. *Just one more day*, I told myself. *Get through one more day, then you can fly home and you won't have to get back out again, ever, if you don't want to.*

When day three arrived, I wasn't as terrified to go downstairs. I knew what was waiting for me—hugs, and people, and more hugs. *Get through one more day and you're home free*, I mused.

The day proceeded with less effort than the prior two days. Then something totally unexpected happened. During the event, an opportunity to take part in a country transformation trip was presented to the attendees. I didn't know what it meant, but I was intrigued. Only 250 coaches would be allowed to participate, and they would be traveling to Costa Rica.

The opportunity sounded exciting. It was a chance to experience something I never thought I could do, so I signed up. As soon as I registered to attend, I started hyperventilating. *What have I done?* I screamed silently. It was a sudden case of buyer's remorse.

My mind began racing…. H*ow would I ever get on a plane and travel internationally?* I immediately told myself I didn't have to go and could always change my mind.

As the time approached to leave for the trip, my stomach churned, and I asked myself, *What is the one thing I CAN do?* I could pack. It didn't mean anything because I could always unpack.

When the day came for me to go to the airport, anxiety engulfed me. *Okay,* I thought. *What is the one thing I CAN do?* I could shower and finish packing.

With that done, *Now, what is the one thing I CAN do?* Drive to the airport. On and on, the conversation was the same. *What is one thing I CAN do?* And each time, I focused on the moment and the next step I needed to take. Before long, I sat at the gate, waiting for my departure. Before I knew it, I sat on the plane, heading toward the connecting flight that would take me to Costa Rica.

When I stepped off the plane in another country, I couldn't believe it! *My first international flight!* There I was, taking this journey one step at a time.

While there, all my anxiety, all my fear melted away. I was among friends, making connections, making a difference, and having the time of my life.

Empowered by this newfound freedom, I altered my traveling plans, booked a tour, and stayed an extra day to enjoy the country. It was remarkable, and I came home transformed.

And what a transformation! I didn't hesitate to jump in the car and drive to conferences. First, I drove to Louisville, Kentucky. Then Dallas, Texas. Then multiple trips to Atlanta, Georgia. The world was opening up to me, and I was ready to see and experience it.

And after three years, here I stood. On top of a platform sixty feet in the air. It was not an easy task to get there. I was coached with the expectations that I did not have to do that challenge. I could opt for a course not so far off the ground, but my heart wanted to experience the biggest obstacle on the course.

When my group reached the challenge, we got our safety equipment on and received some training on the ground. All of a sudden, we stood at the base of the cargo net. I stopped breathing.

I knew the battle that would soon rage in my mind. *I can't, I can't, I can't. Well, what is the one thing I CAN do?* I can take a step. I purposely positioned myself in the middle of the group. Watching others climb the cargo net gave me confidence that I could do it as well. Having people behind me gave me the accountability that others were waiting on me to get to the platform so they could also climb and experience this challenge.

What CAN I do? Take one step. *Now what?* Take another step. Then another and another and another. I was completely focused on the task at hand, and step by step, I climbed the cargo net. Finally, I heard a voice from above say, "Stop." I looked up, and there was a photographer pointing his camera at me, telling me to smile. I remember thinking, *Wait, what? I'm almost sixty feet in the air, I'm trying to make it to the top without completely freaking out, and you want me to smile? Well, okay, Mr. photographer.* I smiled, quickly resumed my focus, and climbed the last few steps to the platform.

Do you know how well-meaning people tell those who are afraid of heights to not look down? I think I heard some voice in my head saying those words. *Don't look down.* I looked down. Then something totally unexpected happened. I was suddenly aware I wasn't afraid. I looked down again. I looked up. I looked out at the view. Others were doing other challenges at different locations. It was so beautiful that I grabbed my phone and started taking pictures and selfies. *How did I get here?* I asked myself. Simple. One step at a time.

AFTER THE ENTIRE GROUP made it to the platform, we partnered up and made our way across one challenging section after another, including walking on a wire to get to the next platform. It was challenging, but I was determined to make it across. I did it, with friends encouraging my every step. They had no idea the internal war I fought as I took each step across the course.

At the end, we had to step off the final platform backwards and lower ourselves to the ground. I refused to do it until all that was left was the photographer, our guide, and me. Then there was no choice but to trust and take that final step. I took a deep breath and stepped off the platform.

When my feet hit the ground, I felt like I was ten feet tall. I had done it. I stepped up to that challenge, and taking one step at a time, I did something I never imagined I could or would ever do. And then it hit me. *What other things am I letting fear keep me from doing?* That was my aha moment, my turning point. It began by signing up for a certification so I could work from home, and finding myself on a rope course, six feet in the air just three years later.

What are you afraid of, friend? Is there something you want to do in your life, but, like me, you let fear prevent you from taking that first step? What would it cost you to take a step? What is it costing you to not take that step?

For so many years, I had let fear beat me down. Afraid of people, of what they would think of me, afraid that somehow I wouldn't measure up to their expectations and feel humiliated. If we had met each other before I began my journey and you met me again today, I guarantee you wouldn't think I was the same person. My life has been completely transformed.

Now, I travel internationally, training facilitators how to conduct round tables about leadership values. I've been to Paraguay and most recently, to the Dominican Republic. I've spoken with people from various walks of life, including children, and I get to tell them briefly about my journey. From being afraid of people to standing before them as an example of how they can change their lives.

John C. Maxwell says, "Once you taste significance, success never satisfies."

No longer fearful of people and what they might think of me, I'm finally living that life of significance.

It started with one step.

Take the first step, my friend. I believe in you.

About Karen

KAREN SILIVEN-MONNIER is an international trainer, speaker, and coach. She helps businesses with leadership challenges and assists caregivers in navigating life challenges. An avid hiker, she enjoys being in nature and often draws inspiration from the various trails she hikes in the Ozarks. She resides in Missouri with various animals and is a self-taught artist specializing in pyrography. Designs by Fire can be seen at www.Dukoda.com

CONNECT WITH KAREN

- Website: dukoda.com
- www.ksmonnier.com
- Email: karen@dukoda.com

Kim Bark White

ROLLER COASTER RIDE OF GRIEF

I HATE ROLLER COASTERS! I can't stand the feeling of my heart dropping out of my chest, over and over again. There's no thrill in it for me. Instead, I'm petrified. The anticipation of each incline and descent makes my heart race and nausea takes over. I swear I'm going to die riding one!

Who would I turn to when life as I knew it was shattered because I was forced to ride that roller coaster? When my dad and brother died suddenly, I no longer had my two protectors with me. I felt like someone had shoved me onto the one harnessless seat, and all I could do was try to hang on, ride, and eventually freefall, crashing to the ground with such an impact that I landed in a deep pit. I wasn't prepared for this horrific ride; how could I be?

My dad and my brother were my world. I could count on them from day one. They spent their lives loving, supporting, guiding, encouraging, and protecting me. They were my rocks. One day they were here, and just like that, they were not. *How would I survive without the two greatest men in my life?*

My brother Duane was my ride or die, my best friend, and my biggest fan. He was a coach, school administrator, a man of faith, and lived to make life better for others. Duane was two years older, and spent his life doting on me, looking at me with pure adoration. Our love was immense; a connection deep within our souls. We didn't fight or argue; we relied on each other. "I got your back, Sis," was spoken thousands of times, a promise never broken. Duane made sure I had a locker next to his in high school—protection by proximity. He screened my potential dates, making sure his standards for his "Li'l Sis" were met. Duane would drop everything to be there for me if I needed him, even on his wedding day. During the gift opening, Duane excused himself from his bride, Pam, to come to my rescue. I was crying hysterically because I was "losing" him. Duane bear-hugged me, kissed my forehead, and reassured me of his love, saying he'd be there for me.

Dad was a kind, gentle soul, with a quiet demeanor. He spent his life teaching and coaching. He taught me biology, and how to be a compassionate and respectful human being. I am *the* epitome of a daddy's girl. As a toddler, I packed my blankie in his sleeping bag when he left for graduate school, so he wouldn't miss me. We went trout fishing; he fished, and I traipsed along beside him. Most nights, we'd sit chatting over a bowl of ice cream. I'd spend weekends at school with him helping make mimeographed copies; the sound as the crank pushed each paper through will forever be priceless memories. A glass bottle of pop from the teachers' lounge was our treat when we were done. Every day for four years, I rode to school with Dad, and I'll always treasure those moments. Dad was proud to escort me onto the football field, standing at the 50-yard line, as the PA system recognized me as sophomore homecoming representative. At that moment, the half-time huddle with his fellow coaches and players wasn't important. That sense of pride was outshined on my wedding day; being father of the bride would only occur once! As we awaited our entrance, Dad looked toward my husband-to-be, whispering, "You better take care of her; I loved her first." There's nothing my dad wouldn't do for me, and vice versa. Dad was my knight in shining armor.

Our mutual love and respect ran deep. This was put to the test in May 2017. Mom, Duane, and I had to make the tough decision that dad would need to go to a memory care unit. I had to love dad enough to convince him to go. Dad was lying on the emergency room bed, and I was sitting on the stool beside him. I held his hands tightly, looked into his brown eyes, and said, "Dad, can you do this for me? Can you let Mom and me drive you?" He squeezed my hands, looked at me and said, "I'll do anything for you." Complete trust. As we left town, we drove through the A&W and had that familiar bowl of ice cream together. As time passed, I slowly watched my dad, my hero, become someone I didn't know. From his standpoint, I was becoming someone he no longer recognized either. Two-sided verbal conversations eventually turned into one-sided conversations. Eyes that were once filled with life and stories became eyes with blank stares. His memory faded, but the power of touch didn't. Unspoken love remained. Unfortunately, the grieving process with dementia lingers while your loved one is still alive. That sucks! The longest goodbye kind of grief never really allows you time to catch your breath before the next twist, turn, or freefall comes.

We certainly weren't seeking thrill rides; we just wanted more time together. What could happen to take me from being a whole person, enjoying life, to becoming shattered pieces in a deep hole under roller coaster ruins? Buckle up. You're about to ride with me through 2020 as I share the peaks and valleys of my journey through grief.

July 2020, in the midst of the COVID-19 pandemic, three family members were COVID positive and hospitalized. Unfortunately, Duane ended up testing positive too. Wanting to spare our mom from worry, he said,

"Don't tell her yet," hoping it would be a mild case. Each day, I noticed his breathing was becoming more labored during our chats. "Get to the doctor," I begged. He ignored my concerns. *If he was hospitalized, how could he take care of his loved ones?* Duane was admitted to the hospital and immediately taken to the intensive care unit (ICU). My world shook, but we continued to talk via phone and FaceTime. He was still protecting me, saying he'd be fine. Our conversations continued, reassuring each other of our love. He promised he'd be okay. I promised I'd have his back and help him fight. My heart was heavy, my gut felt nauseous. He was three hours away, and I felt helpless. I wanted to be in that ICU holding his hand and hugging him. This time, I wanted to comfort *him* with a kiss on the forehead. COVID regulations dictated I couldn't be there. Being a woman of faith, I prayed, remaining hopeful he'd in fact be okay. Days became weeks, and things weren't improving. Our conversations continued but decreased in length. His energy was consumed with breathing. I was petrified and didn't know what to expect. I knew a fast decline could happen at any moment, leaving me dizzy and disoriented.

In early August, my brother and I had our last two-way conversation, minutes before he was placed on a ventilator and in an induced coma. I tried to be brave and not cry when he asked me for a favor. "Absolutely. What do you need?" "Be careful. Don't let your guard down. This COVID is serious shit! Promise me you'll take care of yourself and be safe." We each said, "I love you." I told him he'd come through this; it was only temporary so he could get stronger. I said I'd be BarkStrong (our family motto), keep my faith, and continue praying. I reassured him I'd be there for Mom and both our families. Good-bye wasn't said. Our last words were, "Love ya, Sis." "Love ya too, Big Bro."

In late August, Duane needed a tracheostomy and feeding tube. I lived an all-consuming, numbed life, riding that emotional roller coaster. Duane's medical team said things looked grim. Then, miracles would happen; his numbers would improve, and he'd nod to answer the nurses' questions, all while still in a medically induced coma. This can only be explained by God's grace. People were praying for Duane nonstop.

The numerous ups and downs were taking a toll on our entire family. Dad's stage of dementia didn't allow him to understand what was happening. During this time, I'd go into work intermittently. I was tied to my phone waiting for life altering news. I'd either be stepping off my roller coaster, safe and sound, or I'd be experiencing more twists, turns, and devastating falls. I put my life on hold, obsessed with waiting for updates of Duane's condition. On the outside, I looked mostly the same, but inside, I was crumbling.

All of September, Duane's health fluctuated. I'd pray, thanking God for His healing hands, and the next phone calls would shatter me as Duane's numbers plummeted and his medical team said they were running out of options. I experienced these extremes for days on end. A friend of mine said it best. "Pray fervently, Kim." I did! As days turned into weeks, and weeks into months, I dug deeper into my faith, trusting God. PrayStrong. StayStrong. BarkStrong. Mid-September, in the middle of the night, I got *that* call from Pam. "Come to the hospital immediately." My husband, my mom, and I headed for the hospital three hours away. I prayed the whole way there. Actually, I begged. I begged for the miracle that I'd get Duane back as I knew him.

COVID stipulations said no visitors, but somehow, Pam got permission. Although it broke my heart to see him in a coma, lying in that ICU bed with tubes and monitors everywhere, finally being with him was a comfort. For ninety minutes, I talked to him, held his hand, prayed over him, and kissed his head. More prayers on the way home. "Please God, don't take my brother from me." We finished out September getting glimpses of miracles, and then shattering blows that pulled the rug out from under us, forcing another freefall drop.

On October 6th, Pam called; their family had decided to turn off the ventilator. There were no more options. He had suffered long enough. For three months, Duane fought the fight to no avail. As I heard those words, my heart shattered. They literally took my breath away. *How will I live without him?* Sitting in my living room, embraced by my mom and husband, on October 7th, by video call we watched Duane's last ventilated breath. My world was slowly crumbling. I didn't have my protector, my everything, to hold me in that moment. There was no bottom to that deep pit; I just kept falling. Duane's passing was devastating. Not physically being with him at that moment was unbearable, bringing oppressive sadness and physical pain. I cried; sometimes tears rolled uncontrollably down my face, and other times, my body shook as if I was crying, but no tears flowed. God hears tears as well as spoken words. I sank even lower. I went through the motions, one foot in front of the other, but I was numb. It felt paralyzing. "Keep the Faith, Kim," I heard. I tried. I had so many talks with God. I didn't volunteer to go on that horrendous roller coaster ride. *How will I navigate the rest of my life?*

Another gut punch came in November. *I haven't even exited the roller coaster area; how could I be riding it again?* In the midst of my grieving and living life without Duane, Mom got news from the nursing home that Dad had COVID. More jolting. It had been months since I'd been able to be with Dad because of COVID restrictions.

On December 3rd, with my family beside me, we had a video call with Dad, telling him we loved him, saying our goodbyes. That evening, my dad took his last earthly breath. My hero was gone. The finality was intensified, I couldn't be with him. Damn you, COVID! That's twice you've done this to me! I hate COVID *and* roller coasters!

For the majority of the fall, I was a walking zombie and rarely at my job. Instead I was wallowing in the bottomless pit. I tried keeping God close, but that was fading too. God didn't give up on me. "Walk closer, Kim. You're not alone. I'll never leave you. I'm right here in the eye of your storm." Christmas came. I was quarantined. My first Christmas without Duane and Dad and I'm alone in my house, shattered and numb. On December 28th, I was in an ambulance, with stroke-like symptoms, heading to a hospital eighty miles away. Again, alone and scared. More praying, leaning on God. Thankfully, it wasn't a stroke. But emotionally, I was sinking further into the pit. I was shutting down. I thought I'd die from the intensity of it all. Physical concerns were now adding to my emotional deterioration. I weighed what I weighed in middle school, began losing my hair, and lost my zest for life. Rock bottom was a horrible place. I needed to find a way to start climbing out.

I took a leave of absence from work in January and spent my days sleeping, praying, talking to my bereavement counselor, and reading every book on grief I could find. There's no how-to manual for grief; it's a personal journey. God placed family and friends in my life to support and love me, even when I tried to push them away.

In February, I went back to teaching. That was short-lived when *I* got COVID. Extremely sick and needing an infusion, I wondered, *Will COVID kill me too?* Life had knocked me down for eight grueling months. *Is there seriously no bottom to this pit?* Beaten down and broken, it seemed impossible to get up. *Who could possibly take me from emptiness to wanting to enjoy life again at its fullest?*

2020 was the most devastating year of my life. Fifty percent of my immediate family was taken from me in less than two months. During Duane's ICU ordeal, I told people he'd come out of it, having a testimony to share about how big his God was! Little did I know that God had a different plan. (Jeremiah 29:11). God had a purpose for my pain and was preparing me to share my story of "test to testimony." God was making me stronger in my faith so I *could* share it with others. God was placing people in my life, so when I was ready, I would make a difference for others' grief journeys. God provided me with *everything* I needed at *exactly* the right time. God needed me and my story to show others what faith is all about. "Your ministry is found where you've been broken. Your testimony is where you've been restored" (author unknown). I've always believed in God and known about prayer and God's Word.

God was saying, "Kim, do more than talk the talk. Walk more fully in your walk. Tell people, 'I was here, a broken soul, now I'm telling my story with God by my side.'" My family and friends tried to pull me out of the deep hole left from the roller coaster wreckage but couldn't. *I* couldn't even "will" myself out; it was God's grace that allowed me to rise above my brokenness. I was given a pile of heavy rocks. I could continue floundering in it, or I could paint them, mold them, and turn them into something beautiful. I realized *my* pile of rocks could be something beautiful to help others along their grief journey.

> *"The final stage of healing is using what happens to you to help other people."* —Gloria Steinem

The climb out of that hole was tough. There was a lot of wreckage to sort through. Healing through grief is an ebb and flow journey. Thankfully, my one constant was God. I prayed for hope, joy, and peace to return to my life. Before this happened, I had faith, but wasn't growing in my faith or sharing it with others. I was sitting in junkyard tires filled with slimy, stagnant water. God used 2020 to dump out the sludge water and refill me with His living water. I've been growing in my faith, and now I'm doing what God placed in my heart. I'm sharing it with others by telling my story. If it can help others walk closer to God as they journey through grief, then my pain was not in vain. Life threw me back-to-back, gut-wrenching punches that were knockouts in my ring of life. With God's grace, I'm back in the ring with my scars, bruises, and tatteredness. I'm sharing in the hope that others will be inspired, take that leap of faith, and trust God. I still have moments and days of sadness, tears, and a heavy heart. However, I'm back! I have hope in my life again. I have a loving God who will always be by my side, no matter what storms of life are ahead of me.

Although the greatest thing I miss is the essence of us, I've found that part of accepting the loss of these two incredible men includes honoring Dad and

Duane daily. Thousands of beautiful memories are etched in my mind. I don't look at the 50-yard line without thoughts of my two football coaches. I don't walk into the teachers' lounge without thinking of the impact they both had on countless lives as educators. I don't sit with a bowl of ice cream without that glimmer in my eye. I don't hear the word Sis without being grateful for the love I was blessed to experience. Dad, Duane, and God are my tripod in Heaven. Although they're not physically here with me, I'm reminded daily they're always by my side, guiding me.

My family and I survived the unimaginable. We are BarkStrong!

About Kim

KIM BARK WHITE lives in Wisconsin with her husband. They have three adult children and four grandchildren. Kim is retired from her twenty-seven-year career as an elementary teacher. Kim now has a business, *Mindful Empowerment*, where she is a tutor, mindfulness coach, reiki master, and life mentor. She helps others dealing with grief by facilitating a grief support group. Kim inspires and empowers others to become the best version of themselves. Kim's ability to have a positive impact on others is driven by her compassion, understanding, and genuine concern for others.

In Kim's leisure moments, she enjoys spending time with her family, boating, reading, and taking walks. You can find Kim somewhere between inspiring others and improving herself.

Faith is a big part of Kim's life. Follow Kim on her grief journey as she walks you through her test to testimony. With God's grace, Kim shares her story in the hope of helping those who are working their way through grief to see that God's plans are always greater than ours. From pain to purpose, Kim is rising above her brokenness, and you can too.

CONNECT WITH KIM

- Facebook: MindfulEmpowermentkw

IN GRATITUDE

THANK YOU TO:

Zach Baer, the love of my life, who continuously loves me, supports me, and encourages me to live my life with purpose and intention every day while in service to others.

Chan Bush, my dad, who loves me and always encourages me to go after my dreams.

To each of the women authors in this book, thank you for trusting me, for being vulnerable by sharing your immensely personal stories, and for unleashing the *badass within*. You are all truly inspiring.

Amy Collette, who is one badass publisher who continues to encourage me to share my story and help others do the same. And to the amazing publishing team for working endlessly on this amazing project.

Victoria Wolf, our cover designer who was able to capture what it means to release the *badass within* with grace, beauty, and power.

Dr. Shellie Hipsky for being a positive light and badass role model. I am honored to call you friend and grateful for your contribution to the world.

Michelle Mras, my mentor and now friend, who has always pushed me to continue reaching for new heights. Because of you, I have learned to live unapologetically.

To both Mama Ellen and Mama Peggy, thank you for your support, love and encouragement while reminding me that I am enough. Your wisdom has helped keep me grounded while reaching for the stars. I love you both as you are family.

To my family and friends. Thank you for supporting and encouraging me to always share my story, speak up, and continue giving others a safe space to do the same. I am forever thankful.

RESOURCES

National Domestic Violence Hotline
1-800-799-7233
https://www.thehotline.org/

ERIN BAER

To book Erin, go to https://erinbaer.com

Charities that Erin Baer (Beaten to Badass) supports
- Star Sweeper: Advancing Women's Voices http://starsweeper.org
- Global Sisterhood http://globalsisterhoodonline.org
- Family Tree https://www.thefamilytree.org/

ABOUT THE BEATEN TO BADASS ORGANIZATION

Erin Baer is the founder of the organization Beaten to Badass, which is dedicated to empowering those who have been beaten down by life to become the badass they were always meant to be. Whether it be by domestic violence, sexual assault, bullying, abandonment, infertility, or however life beats you down, Beaten to Badass is there to *start the conversation, raise awareness, give back, and implement change.*

To learn more or to get your copy of *From Beaten to Badass*, visit: beatentobadass.com

Contact Erin Baer at: erin@beatentobadass.com

THE MAKE AN IMPACT MISSION

How to get involved: In 2020, Beaten to Badass had a goal to put a copy of *From Beaten to Badass* in every shelter across Colorado while expanding nationwide in the USA, to give others hope and show them that they too are a Badass! That goal will continue until the book is in every shelter in the nation.

From Beaten to Badass: My journey of broken blessings and how I became my own hero was released on October 25, 2019, during National Domestic Violence Awareness Month in honor of all the victims and survivors of domestic violence/abuse and sexual assault. As a survivor myself, I promised that if I was ever in a position to give back, I would! I have made it my mission to do that and more. With every book sold, a portion goes back to organizations dedicated to empowering victims and survivors of domestic violence/abuse and sexual assault. In Colorado alone, there are 59 organizations that provide domestic violence programs at some level and within the United States and Canada there are 2,859 organizations.

—Erin Baer

To learn more or to get involved, visit: beatentobadass.com

ABOUT THE AUTHOR

ERIN BAER, founder of Beaten to Badass, is herself a survivor of domestic violence and sexual assault. Beaten to Badass is dedicated to empowering women to become their own hero.

Erin began telling others her story of grace and grit on her road to recovery. This sharing of her personal story became the basis for her first book, *From Beaten to Badass*. The powerfully worded personal memoir gives readers the strength, hope, and courage to keep going and become the *badass* they were always meant to be.

Seeing women being silenced for wanting to be strong, courageous, and proud of who they are while moving on from feeling beaten down by life, Erin decided to be a positive voice providing an example whereby circumstances do not define us and that we, too, can be our own heroes. Through her writing, coaching, and speaking, Erin encourages women to look within where they will find their power to unleash the *badass within*.

Erin holds her BSBA in Business Administration from Rockhurst University and an MBA in Business Management from Avila University. Erin is now a thriving entrepreneurial *badass* who lives her passions as a best-selling author, speaker, and coach. She has contributed to many book collaborations, including *Hold My Crown, Overcoming Heart Blocks,* and *Healing and Growth.* As with all of Erin's projects, a portion of the proceeds go to empowering women's charities. She lives in Colorado with her husband, Zach and their four cats, Taco, Kodak, Leela, and Breckenridge.

CONNECT WITH ERIN

ErinBaer.com and BeatentoBadass.com

Facebook: erinbaerbadass and beatentobadass

Instagram: coach_erinbaer and beatentobadass

LinkedIn: erinbaerbadass

Linktr.ee/erinbaer

FROM BEATEN TO BADASS

By Erin Baer

RAPED, BEATEN, NEARLY KILLED, bullied, abandoned, abused and broken. She shouldn't have survived, but she did. Ultimately, she became a strong, independent woman who possesses qualities that are a perfect match for what life throws her way. Erin gained insight and resilience while traveling through peaks and valleys with the help of mentors, friends, parents, and coaches, who all made a difference in her life.

Erin's story shows how a strong woman stands tall like a tree, rooted to her beliefs. Just when you think you may break, you can bend with the wind to find another success. Erin lives with the most energetic and positive outlook on life whose life purpose is to confront the "elephants in the room" and give all women strength. By inspiring and motivating, she teaches them to leverage all of what life throws their way to bring out the powerful women they truly are.

www.ingramcontent.com/pod-product-compliance
Lightning Source LLC
Chambersburg PA
CBHW071206160426
43196CB00011B/2212